New Instant
Pot Cookbook for
Beginners 2025

2000+ Days Easy and Amazing Instant Pot Recipes Includes soups, Dinners, Breakfasts and Delicious Desserts | Step by Step Beginners Guide

Susan J. Melendy

TABLE OF

CONTENTS

Introduction To The Instant Pot: A Game-Changer In The Kitchen

In today's fast-paced world, the need for time-saving solutions in the kitchen has never been greater. Introducing the Instant Pot, a multifunctional kitchen appliance that has transformed the way we prepare food. What started as a programmable pressure cooker has evolved into an all-in-one cooking tool capable of sautéing, steaming, slow cooking, and more. This kitchen companion has found a place in homes worldwide, offering convenience without compromising the quality of the food we prepare.

At first glance, the Instant Pot may seem like just another pressure cooker, but its versatility extends far beyond that. Designed to save time while enhancing the flavors of your favorite dishes, the Instant Pot is a must-have for anyone looking to simplify their cooking experience. Whether you're cooking a quick weeknight dinner or preparing a more elaborate meal, this kitchen gadget can handle it all.

What is an Instant Pot?

An Instant Pot is a multi-functional electric cooker that combines the capabilities of several kitchen appliances in one device. At its core, it is a pressure cooker that uses high-pressure steam to cook food faster than traditional cooking methods. However, it can also function as a slow cooker, rice cooker, steamer, yogurt maker, and even a sauté pan. The unique combination of features makes the Instant Pot an essential tool for anyone who wants to streamline meal preparation.

The appliance typically comes with a variety of preset cooking modes for different types of dishes, allowing users to easily select the best settings for their needs. These presets eliminate much of the guesswork, providing a straightforward, user-friendly cooking experience.

Why Choose an Instant Pot for Cooking?

There are many reasons to consider adding an Instant Pot to your kitchen arsenal. Here are a few key benefits that make it stand out from other cooking appliances:

1. Time-Saving Efficiency: In today's busy world, time is of the essence, and the Instant Pot is a huge time-saver. By using pressure cooking, the Instant Pot dramatically reduces cooking time for many recipes, allowing meals that would normally take hours on the stove or in the oven to be prepared in a fraction of the time. For example, a beef stew that would traditionally simmer for several hours on the stovetop can be cooked in just 40 minutes using the Instant Pot.

2. Multi-functionality and Versatility: The Instant Pot can perform the functions of several different kitchen appliances. It serves as a pressure cooker, slow cooker, rice cooker, yogurt maker, steamer, and even a sauté pan. For those with limited kitchen space or those looking to minimize the number of gadgets in their home, the Instant Pot is the perfect solution.

3. Flavor Infusion: Thanks to its sealed cooking environment, the Instant Pot locks in flavors and moisture. As food is cooked under pressure, the flavors are absorbed more deeply, resulting in richer, more intense dishes. It's like slow cooking in a fraction of the time, which is especially beneficial for meats, stews, and soups.

4. Ease of Use: One of the Instant Pot's most attractive features is its simplicity. With its easy-to-use interface and preset cooking programs, even a beginner cook can quickly get started. Simply add the ingredients, select the program, and let the Instant Pot do the rest.

5. Healthier Meals: The Instant Pot is perfect for preparing healthy meals because it retains more

nutrients compared to traditional cooking methods. The sealed environment ensures that vitamins and minerals are preserved in the food. Additionally, it allows you to cook with less oil or fat, making it ideal for those following a healthier diet.

What the Instant Pot Can Do and What It Cannot Do

The Instant Pot is an incredibly versatile appliance, but it's essential to understand its limits. Here's a breakdown of what the Instant Pot excels at and what it may not be the best tool for:

What the Instant Pot Can Do

1. Pressure Cook: The Instant Pot excels at cooking foods quickly using high-pressure steam. This is especially useful for tougher cuts of meat, beans, rice, and grains.
2. Slow Cook: The Instant Pot also functions as a slow cooker, allowing you to prepare soups, stews, and braises with long, low heat over several hours.
3. Sautéing: The sauté function is ideal for browning meat, onions, garlic, and other ingredients before pressure cooking, enhancing the overall flavor of your dish.
4. Steaming: The Instant Pot's steaming function works well for vegetables, seafood, and even dumplings.
5. Rice Cooking: The Instant Pot does a great job cooking rice and other grains to perfection without having to monitor it constantly.
6. Yogurt Making: The Instant Pot can also be used to make yogurt, making it a great tool for those who prefer homemade, fresh yogurt.

What the Instant Pot Cannot Do

1. Bake Traditional Cakes: While it's possible to make some desserts, such as cheesecake, in the Instant Pot, traditional cakes that require baking won't come out the same way as in a conventional oven. The Instant Pot uses steam for cooking, which differs from dry heat in a traditional oven.
2. Grilling: The Instant Pot cannot replace a grill for cooking foods like steaks, burgers, or vegetables with that crispy, charred texture.
3. Roasting: While it can cook many roasted dishes, it doesn't give you the same caramelized and crispy exterior you might expect from an oven-roasted dish.

Instant Pot Cleaning and Maintenance

To keep your Instant Pot in top working condition and extend its lifespan, regular cleaning and maintenance are crucial. Here's a step-by-step guide:

1. Clean the Lid: After every use, make sure to clean the lid. Remove the sealing ring and wash it thoroughly. The sealing ring can sometimes retain odors, so it's important to clean it well. You can also soak it in vinegar or lemon juice to eliminate any lingering smells.
2. Clean the Inner Pot: The inner pot is typically non-stick and should be washed with warm, soapy water. Avoid using abrasive sponges or scrubbers, as they can damage the coating. You can also put it in the dishwasher if it's dishwasher-safe.
3. Clean the Steam Release Valve: The steam release valve can sometimes accumulate food particles, which can affect the functioning of the Instant Pot. Check and clean it regularly with a soft brush or cloth to prevent clogging.
4. Check the Float Valve: The float valve is responsible for controlling the pressure inside the pot. Make sure it's clean and free from debris to ensure proper pressure release.
5. Regularly Inspect the Power Cord: Before each use, inspect the power cord for any visible signs of wear or damage. If you notice any issues, contact the manufacturer or consider replacing it.

Tips and Tricks for Using Your Instant Pot

To make the most of your Instant Pot, here are some helpful tips and tricks:

- Understand the Functions: Before you start cooking, get familiar with the different buttons and functions on your Instant Pot. Understanding how to use the pressure release valve, how to set cooking times, and when to use different modes will ensure that your cooking goes smoothly.
- Use Enough Liquid: Pressure cooking relies on steam, so always ensure you use enough liquid (usually 1 to 1.5 cups) to build pressure. Not enough liquid can cause the Instant Pot to fail to pressurize properly.
- Sauté First for Extra Flavor: Using the sauté function

before pressure cooking can develop deep, rich flavors in your dish. Brown meats, onions, and garlic before setting the Instant Pot to cook under pressure to give your meal an extra flavor boost.

- Use the Pot-in-Pot Method: The pot-in-pot method is a great way to cook multiple items at once. You can stack containers inside your Instant Pot to cook side dishes, rice, or desserts while your main dish is cooking. This method can save time and make meal prep even easier.
- Use Natural Pressure Release for Delicate Foods: For delicate foods like fish or dairy-based dishes, it's best to use natural pressure release (NPR). This allows the pressure to come down slowly, preventing the food from being overcooked or becoming mushy.
- Layer Your Ingredients: When cooking dishes with multiple ingredients, layer the heavier, denser items (like potatoes or meat) at the bottom and lighter items (like vegetables) on top. This ensures that everything cooks evenly.
- Regular Maintenance: Clean your Instant Pot regularly to maintain its performance. Make sure to check the sealing ring, steam release valve, and the inner pot after every use.

Recipes You Can Cook with the Instant Pot

The Instant Pot opens up a world of culinary possibilities. Here are some delicious dishes you can easily make with it:

1. Beef Stew: In just under an hour, the Instant Pot can transform tough cuts of beef into tender, flavorful stew. Combine chunks of beef with vegetables, herbs, and broth, and let the Instant Pot do the work.
2. Chicken Tikka Masala: This classic Indian dish becomes a breeze in the Instant Pot. Marinate the chicken in yogurt and spices, pressure cook it, and then simmer in a creamy tomato-based sauce for a rich, flavorful meal.
3. Risotto: Forget standing over the stove stirring for hours. The Instant Pot can cook a creamy, delicious risotto in under 30 minutes, allowing you to enjoy this Italian classic without the hassle.
4. Chili: Whether you like it spicy or mild, the Instant Pot can cook a hearty chili in no time. Combine beans, ground beef, tomatoes, and spices, and let the Instant Pot pressure cook everything to perfection. The result is a flavorful, thick chili that's ready in under an hour.
5. Rice and Beans: A classic, simple dish made easy in the Instant Pot.

The pressure cooker function allows you to cook dried beans and rice together, all while infusing them with flavor in half the time it would take using traditional methods.

6. Pulled Pork: For a tender and juicy pulled pork, the Instant Pot is the way to go. Cook a pork shoulder with your favorite BBQ seasonings, and in less than two hours, you'll have perfectly shredded pork ready for sandwiches, tacos, or just a hearty meal.
7. Yogurt: The Instant Pot makes yogurt-making a breeze. With a yogurt function, you can create creamy, fresh yogurt at home, customized with your preferred sweetness or flavorings. No need to buy store-bought yogurt ever again!
8. Hard-Boiled Eggs: Perfectly cooked hard-boiled eggs are incredibly easy to make in the Instant Pot. With just a bit of water and a few minutes of cooking time, you'll have perfectly cooked eggs every time. It's the ultimate hack for meal prepping.
9. Mac and Cheese: Mac and cheese doesn't get any easier than in the Instant Pot. The noodles, cheese, milk, and butter cook together in one pot, resulting in a creamy and comforting dish in under 20 minutes.
10. Cheesecake: Believe it or not, the Instant Pot is an excellent tool for making cheesecakes. It uses a gentle, steam-based cooking method that ensures a smooth, creamy texture without worrying about cracks. It's an ideal dessert for any special occasion.

Tips for Instant Pot Success

- Don't Overcrowd the Pot: The Instant Pot works best when there's enough room for steam and pressure to build. Avoid overfilling it, and leave a little space at the top to ensure even cooking.
- Adjust Cooking Time Based on Altitude: If you live at a high altitude, you may need to adjust the cooking

3. Keep the Vent Clear: Ensure that the steam release valve and vent are clean and unobstructed. If these areas are blocked, it can lead to unsafe pressure levels and cooking malfunctions.

4. Be Cautious of Steam: The Instant Pot releases steam at high temperatures, especially during quick release. Always use a towel or oven mitt to carefully turn the steam release valve to avoid burns.

5. Use the Right Ingredients: Some ingredients, such as dairy or delicate vegetables, require careful attention when cooking in the Instant Pot. Be sure to read up on the best practices for cooking certain foods to ensure the best results and avoid any cooking mishaps.

time. For every 1,000 feet above sea level, increase the cooking time by about 5 percent.

- Be Mindful of Release Methods: There are two main pressure release methods: quick release and natural release. Quick release involves turning the valve to release pressure immediately after cooking, while natural release lets the pressure gradually decrease on its own. Use natural release for delicate foods and quick release for faster, more robust cooking results.
- Use the Right Amount of Liquid: The Instant Pot relies on steam to build pressure, so always ensure you're using enough liquid. Generally, you'll need at least 1 to 1.5 cups of liquid for the Instant Pot to reach the required pressure.
- Experiment with Different Recipes: The Instant Pot is a versatile kitchen tool, so don't be afraid to experiment with different recipes. Whether you're trying a new dish or adapting an old favorite, the Instant Pot's wide range of features opens the door to endless culinary possibilities.

Instant Pot Safety Tips

While the Instant Pot is designed to be safe and user-friendly, it's essential to follow proper safety protocols when using it. Here are some safety tips to keep in mind:

1. Check the Sealing Ring: Always ensure that the sealing ring is correctly positioned and free of debris. If the sealing ring is not securely in place, the Instant Pot won't reach the necessary pressure for cooking.
2. Don't Force the Lid Open: Never attempt to open the Instant Pot while it's still pressurized. Wait for the pressure to release, either naturally or manually, before opening the lid.

Conclusion

The Instant Pot has undeniably become a staple in kitchens around the world. Its ability to streamline meal prep, save time, and cook a variety of dishes quickly has made it an indispensable tool for busy families and home cooks alike. With its multiple cooking functions, you can create everything from hearty stews to decadent desserts—all in a fraction of the time it would take using traditional methods.

Whether you're new to the Instant Pot or looking for more advanced tips and tricks, there's no shortage of possibilities for what you can cook with this amazing appliance. With a little practice and some creativity, you'll be able to unlock the full potential of your Instant Pot and enjoy delicious, home-cooked meals in no time.

By following the tips, tricks, and safety protocols outlined in this article, you'll be well on your way to becoming an Instant Pot expert. The key is to experiment, learn from experience, and most importantly, have fun with your cooking. With the Instant Pot by your side, you'll be creating impressive meals with ease and discovering new ways to simplify your kitchen routine.

Happy cooking!

Creamy Spinach and Bacon Baked Eggs

Serves: 4 / Prep time: 5 minutes / Cook time: 9 minutes

Ingredients:

- 2 tablespoons unsalted butter, divided
- 1/2 cup diced bacon
- 1/3 cup finely diced shallots
- 1/3 cup chopped spinach leaves
- Pinch of salt
- Pinch of black pepper
- 1/2 cup water
- 1/4 cup heavy cream
- 8 large eggs
- 1 tablespoon chopped fresh chives, for garnish

Instructions:

1. Set the Instant Pot to Sauté and add 1 tablespoon of butter to melt. Add the bacon, cooking for about 4 minutes until crispy. Use a slotted spoon to remove the bacon and place it in a small bowl, setting it aside.
2. Add the remaining tablespoon of butter and the shallots to the pot. Sauté for about 2 minutes until softened, then add the spinach, stirring for 1 minute until it wilts. Season with salt and black pepper, stir, then transfer the spinach to a separate bowl.
3. Carefully drain the pot, reserving the bacon grease. Pour in the water and place the trivet inside the pot.
4. Use a paper towel to lightly coat four ramekins with some of the reserved bacon grease. In each ramekin, add 1 tablespoon of heavy cream, a portion of the bacon, and some spinach. Crack two eggs into each ramekin, keeping the yolks intact. Cover each ramekin with aluminum foil. Arrange two ramekins on the trivet, then stack the other two on top.
5. Secure the lid and set the Instant Pot to Manual on Low Pressure for 2 minutes. Once done, allow a natural pressure release for 5 minutes, then release any remaining pressure and carefully remove the lid.
6. Take the ramekins out and sprinkle with fresh chives for garnish. Serve warm.

Italian Parmesan Baked Eggs

Serves: 1 / Prep time: 5 minutes / Cook time: 10 minutes

Ingredients:

- 1 tablespoon butter, cut into small pieces
- 2 tablespoons low-carb marinara sauce
- 3 eggs
- 2 tablespoons grated Parmesan

- ¼ teaspoon Italian seasoning
- 1 cup water

Instructions:

1. Place butter pieces in an oven-safe bowl, spread marinara sauce over the butter, then crack the eggs over the sauce. Sprinkle with Parmesan and Italian seasoning.
2. Cover the bowl with foil. Add water and place the trivet in the Instant Pot. Position the bowl on the trivet.
3. Secure the lid and select Manual mode, setting to cook for 10 minutes on Low Pressure. Quick-release the pressure once done.
4. Let eggs cool for 5 minutes before serving.

Instant Pot Ranch-Style Coddled Eggs

Serves: 2 / Prep time: 5 minutes / Cook time: 10 minutes

Ingredients:

- 2 teaspoons unsalted butter
- 4 large eggs
- 1 cup cooked black beans, drained (or two-thirds of a 15-ounce can, rinsed and drained)
- Two 7-inch corn or whole-wheat tortillas, warmed
- ½ cup chunky tomato salsa (like Pace)
- 2 cups shredded romaine lettuce
- 1 tablespoon fresh cilantro, chopped
- 2 tablespoons grated Cotija cheese

Instructions:

1. Add 1 cup water to the Instant Pot and set a long-handled silicone steam rack inside. If using a standard rack, create a sling for easy removal.
2. Coat each of four 4-ounce ramekins with ½ teaspoon butter, then crack an egg into each one. Arrange the ramekins on the steam rack in the pot.
3. Secure the lid and set the Pressure Release to Sealing. Select Steam mode and cook for 3 minutes at low pressure (allowing about 5 minutes for pressure buildup).
4. While the eggs cook, warm the beans in a small saucepan over low heat for about 5 minutes, stirring occasionally. Alternatively, microwave the beans for 1 minute and keep covered until serving.
5. After cooking, let the pressure release naturally for 5 minutes, then move the Pressure Release to Venting to release any remaining steam. Carefully lift out the ramekins.
6. Serve by placing a tortilla on each plate, spooning ½

cup beans onto each, and gently releasing two eggs from each ramekin onto the beans. Top with salsa, lettuce, cilantro, and cheese, and serve right away.

Instant Pot Potato and Bacon Omelet

Serves: 6 / Prep time: 15 minutes / Cook time: 20 minutes

Ingredients:

- 3 slices bacon, cooked and crumbled
- 2 cups cooked, shredded potatoes
- ¼ cup minced onion
- ¼ cup minced green bell pepper
- 1 cup egg substitute
- ¼ cup fat-free milk
- ¼ teaspoon salt
- ⅛ teaspoon black pepper
- 1 cup reduced-fat shredded cheddar cheese
- 1 cup water

Instructions:

1. Lightly spray a round baking dish with nonstick spray. Arrange the bacon, potatoes, onion, and bell pepper in the dish.
2. In a bowl, combine egg substitute, milk, salt, and pepper. Pour over the potato mixture.
3. Top with shredded cheese.
4. Pour water into the Instant Pot and place the steaming rack at the bottom. Set the baking dish on top of the rack.
5. Secure the lid, making sure the vent is sealed. Cook on Manual for 20 minutes at high pressure.
6. Allow the pressure to release naturally.
7. Carefully remove the dish, let it stand for 10 minutes, then slice and serve.

Blueberry Oat Mini Muffins

Serves: 7 / Prep time: 12 minutes / Cook time: 10 minutes

Ingredients:

- ½ cup rolled oats
- ¼ cup whole wheat pastry flour or white whole wheat flour
- ½ tablespoon baking powder
- ½ teaspoon ground cardamom or cinnamon
- ⅛ teaspoon kosher salt
- 2 large eggs
- ½ cup plain Greek yogurt
- 2 tablespoons pure maple syrup
- 2 teaspoons olive oil
- ½ teaspoon vanilla extract
- ½ cup frozen blueberries (preferably small wild blueberries)

Instructions:

1. In a large bowl, combine oats, flour, baking powder, cardamom, and salt.
2. In another bowl, whisk eggs, yogurt, maple syrup, oil,

and vanilla.
3. Add the wet Ingredients to the dry mixture and stir just until blended. Fold in blueberries.
4. Spoon the batter into an egg bite mold.
5. Pour 1 cup water into the pressure cooker, place the mold on a wire rack, and lower it into the pot.
6. Lock the lid, set the valve to sealing, and cook on high pressure for 10 minutes.
7. Let pressure release naturally for 10 minutes, then quick-release any remaining pressure.
8. Carefully remove the mold, cool for 5 minutes, and turn out onto a rack. Serve warm or store in the fridge or freezer.

Cheesy Chicken Casserole

Serves: 6 / Prep time: 10 minutes / Cook time: 20 minutes

Ingredients:

- 1 cup ground chicken
- 1 teaspoon olive oil
- 1 teaspoon chili flakes
- 1 teaspoon salt
- 1 cup shredded cheddar cheese
- ½ cup coconut cream

Instructions:

1. Set the Instant Pot to Sauté mode and heat the olive oil. Add the ground chicken, chili flakes, and salt, cooking for about 10 minutes. Stir in the shredded cheese and coconut cream until combined.
2. Lock the lid and select Manual mode, setting the time to cook for 10 minutes on High Pressure. When done, quickly release the pressure. Carefully open the lid.
3. Let the casserole cool for about 10 minutes before serving.

Cynthia's Homemade Yogurt

Serves: 16 / Prep time: 10 minutes / Cook time: 8 hours

Ingredients:

- 1 gallon low-fat milk
- ¼ cup low-fat plain yogurt with live active cultures

Instructions:

1. Pour the milk into the Instant Pot's inner pot.
2. Lock the lid, set the vent to sealing, and press the Yogurt button. Press Adjust until it reads "boil."
3. After about an hour, once the cycle is complete, check the temperature—it should reach 185°F. If not, use the Sauté function to warm it to 185°F.
4. Once heated, unplug the Instant Pot and remove the inner pot, allowing the milk to cool. For quicker cooling, place the pot on a cooling rack or in a basin of cool water. Cool to 110°F.
5. At 110°F, stir in the ¼ cup yogurt. Secure the lid and move the vent to sealing.
6. Press Yogurt and adjust until the screen reads 8:00,

incubating for 8 hours.

7. After 8 hours, refrigerate to chill or proceed to step 8 for straining.

8. For a thicker consistency like Greek yogurt, strain the mixture using a nut milk bag.

Eggs and Smoked Salmon Toasts

Serves: 4 / Prep time: 5 minutes / Cook time: 10 minutes

Ingredients:

- 2 teaspoons unsalted butter
- 4 large eggs
- 4 slices gluten-free or whole-grain rye bread
- ½ cup plain 2% Greek yogurt
- 4 ounces smoked salmon or 1 medium avocado, sliced
- 2 radishes, thinly sliced
- 1 Persian cucumber, thinly sliced
- 1 tablespoon chopped fresh chives
- ¼ teaspoon ground black pepper

Instructions:

1. Pour 1 cup water into the Instant Pot and place a long-handled silicone steam rack inside. (If you don't have one, use a wire steam rack with a homemade sling.)

2. Lightly butter each of four 4-ounce ramekins, then crack an egg into each. Arrange the ramekins on the rack inside the pot.

3. Secure the lid, set the Pressure Release to Sealing, select Steam mode, and cook for 3 minutes on low pressure (allowing 5 minutes for the pot to come to pressure).

4. While the eggs cook, toast the bread slices until golden. Spread each toast with yogurt, then layer on smoked salmon, radishes, and cucumber.

5. When the cooking ends, let the pressure release naturally for 5 minutes, then switch to Venting to release any remaining steam. Carefully lift out the rack with the ramekins.

6. Run a knife around each ramekin to loosen and unmold an egg onto each toast. Sprinkle with chives and black pepper, then serve.

7. Note: For softer yolks, perform a quick release instead of waiting 5 minutes for natural pressure release.

Instant Pot Baked Eggs Casserole

Serves: 8 / Prep time: 15 minutes / Cook time: 20 minutes

Ingredients:

- 1 cup water
- 2 tablespoons trans-fat-free tub margarine, melted
- 1 cup reduced-fat buttermilk baking mix
- 1½ cups fat-free cottage cheese
- 2 teaspoons chopped onion
- 1 teaspoon dried parsley
- ½ cup grated reduced-fat cheddar cheese

- 1 egg, lightly beaten
- 1¼ cups egg substitute
- 1 cup fat-free milk

Instructions:

1. Pour 1 cup of water into the Instant Pot and place the steaming rack at the bottom.

2. Grease a round springform pan that fits into the Instant Pot.

3. Pour melted margarine into the springform pan.

4. In a large bowl, mix the baking mix, cottage cheese, onion, parsley, cheddar, egg, egg substitute, and milk until blended.

5. Pour the mixture over the melted margarine in the pan, stirring slightly to combine.

6. Place the pan on the steam rack, secure the lid, and set the vent to Sealing. Select Manual mode and cook for 20 minutes on High Pressure.

7. Allow the pressure to release naturally.

8. Carefully remove the springform pan and let it sit for 10 minutes before slicing and serving.

Classic Coconut Porridge

Serves: 4 / Prep time: 5 minutes / Cook time: 4 minutes

Ingredients:

- 2 tablespoons coconut oil
- 1 cup full-fat coconut milk
- 2 tablespoons almond flour (blanched)
- 2 tablespoons sugar-free chocolate chips
- 1 cup heavy cream
- ½ cup chopped cashews
- ½ cup chopped pecans
- ½ teaspoon ground cinnamon
- ½ teaspoon erythritol (or to taste)
- ¼ cup unsweetened coconut flakes

Instructions:

1. Set the Instant Pot to Sauté mode, then melt the coconut oil in the pot.

2. Add the coconut milk, 1 cup of filtered water, almond flour, chocolate chips, heavy cream, cashews, pecans, cinnamon, erythritol, and coconut flakes. Stir everything together to combine.

3. Close the lid, set the valve to Sealing, and cancel the Sauté function. Select Manual mode and set to cook for 4 minutes on High Pressure.

4. When finished, carefully perform a quick release by switching the valve to Venting.

5. Open the lid, serve warm, and enjoy!

Crunchy Blueberry Almond Cereal

Serves: 4 / Prep time: 5 minutes / Cook time: 2 minutes

Ingredients:

- ⅓ cup crushed roasted almonds
- ¼ cup almond flour

- ¼ cup unsalted butter, softened
- ¼ cup vanilla egg white protein powder
- 2 tablespoons Swerve sweetener
- 1 teaspoon blueberry extract
- 1 teaspoon ground cinnamon

Instructions:

1. Combine all Ingredients in the Instant Pot and stir until well mixed.
2. Lock the lid, choose Manual mode, and cook for 2 minutes on High Pressure. Allow the pressure to release naturally for 10 minutes, then release any remaining pressure and open the lid.
3. Spread the mixture onto a sheet lined with parchment paper and let it cool completely. It will become crispy as it cools.
4. Serve in bowls and enjoy.

Instant Pot Hard-Boiled Eggs

Serves: 7 / Prep time: 10 minutes / Cook time: 5 minutes

Ingredients:

- 1 cup water
- 6 to 8 eggs

Instructions:

1. Pour the water into the Instant Pot and place a steamer basket or trivet inside. Arrange the eggs in a single layer.
2. Secure the lid, set the valve to Sealing, and select Manual mode, cooking on High Pressure for 5 minutes.
3. Allow a natural release for 5 minutes, then switch to a quick release for any remaining pressure.
4. Transfer the hot eggs to a bowl of cool water to stop the cooking. Peel the cooled eggs or refrigerate unpeeled.

Greek-style Frittata with Kale, Peppers, and Feta

Serves: 6 / Prep time: 5 minutes / Cook time: 45 minutes

Ingredients

- 8 large eggs
- ½ cup plain 2% Greek yogurt
- Fine sea salt
- Freshly ground black pepper
- 2 cups finely shredded kale or baby kale
- One 12-ounce jar roasted red peppers, drained and cut into ¼ by 2-inch strips
- 2 green onions, thinly sliced
- 1 tablespoon fresh dill, chopped
- ⅓ cup crumbled feta cheese
- 6 cups mixed baby greens
- ¾ cup cherry tomatoes, halved
- 2 tablespoons extra-virgin olive oil

Instructions:

1. Pour 1½ cups of water into the Instant Pot. Lightly grease a 7-cup heatproof glass dish with butter or cooking spray.
2. In a bowl, whisk together the eggs, yogurt, ¼ teaspoon salt, and ¼ teaspoon pepper. Fold in the kale, roasted peppers, green onions, dill, and feta cheese.
3. Pour the egg mixture into the greased dish and cover tightly with foil. Place it on a silicone steam rack, then carefully lower it into the Instant Pot.
4. Secure the lid, set the Pressure Release to Sealing, and select Pressure Cook or Manual mode, cooking for 30 minutes on High Pressure. Allow about 15 minutes for pressure buildup.
5. When done, let the pressure release naturally for 10 minutes before switching to Venting to release any remaining steam. Carefully remove the dish, uncover, and let it sit a few minutes to set.
6. In a medium bowl, toss together the mixed greens, tomatoes, and olive oil. Season with salt and pepper to taste.
7. Slice the frittata into six wedges and serve warm with the salad on the side.

Three-Cheese Quiche Cups

Serves: 6 / Prep time: 10 minutes / Cook time: 6 minutes

Ingredients

- 6 eggs, beaten
- 2 tablespoons cream cheese
- 1 teaspoon Italian seasoning
- ¼ cup shredded cheddar cheese
- 3 ounces Monterey Jack cheese, shredded
- 2 ounces mozzarella cheese, shredded
- 1 cup water (for cooking)

Instructions:

1. Pour 1 cup of water into the Instant Pot.
2. In a mixing bowl, whisk together the eggs, cream cheese, Italian seasoning, cheddar, Monterey Jack, and mozzarella until smooth.
3. Divide the mixture evenly into silicone baking cups or molds and place them on the Instant Pot steam rack.
4. Close the lid, set the valve to Sealing, and select Manual mode, setting the time for 6 minutes on High Pressure.
5. When cooking is complete, quickly release the pressure by turning the valve to Venting.
6. Carefully remove the quiche cups and serve warm.

Instant Pot Poached Eggs

Serves: 4 / Prep time: 5 minutes / Cook time: 5 minutes

Ingredients:

- Nonstick cooking spray
- 4 large eggs

Instructions:

1. Lightly coat four cups of a 7-slot silicone egg mold

with nonstick spray. Carefully crack one egg into each prepared cup.
2. Pour 1 cup of water into the Instant Pot. Place the egg mold on a wire rack, then gently lower it into the pot.
3. Close and secure the lid, setting the valve to Sealing.
4. Select High Pressure and cook for 5 minutes.
5. When done, press Cancel and perform a quick pressure release.
6. Once the pin drops, unlock the lid and carefully remove it.
7. Use a rubber spatula or spoon to release each egg from its cup. The whites should be set, while the yolks remain runny.
8. Serve immediately.

Cheesy Bacon Egg Cups

Serves: 4 / Prep time: 5 minutes / Cook time: 7 minutes

Ingredients:
- 6 large eggs
- 2 strips cooked bacon, sliced into ¼-inch pieces
- ½ cup Cheddar cheese, divided
- ¼ teaspoon sea salt
- ¼ teaspoon black pepper
- 1 cup water
- 1 tablespoon chopped fresh flat-leaf parsley

Instructions:
1. Beat the eggs in a small bowl. Mix in the bacon, ¼ cup Cheddar, sea salt, and black pepper. Evenly divide the mixture among four ramekins, covering each loosely with foil.
2. Pour water into the Instant Pot and place a trivet inside. Position two ramekins on the trivet, then carefully stack the remaining two on top.
3. Secure the lid, set to Manual mode, and cook for 7 minutes on High Pressure. After cooking, let the pressure release naturally for 10 minutes, then release any remaining pressure and open the lid.
4. Sprinkle the remaining Cheddar over each egg cup. Lock the lid and let the cheese melt for 2 minutes.
5. Garnish with parsley and serve immediately.

Lettuce-Wrapped Chicken Sliders

Serves: 4 / Prep time: 10 minutes / Cook time: 15 minutes

Ingredients:
- 1 tablespoon butter
- 3 ounces chopped scallions
- 2 cups ground chicken
- ½ teaspoon ground nutmeg
- 1 tablespoon coconut flour
- 1 teaspoon salt
- 1 cup lettuce leaves

Instructions:
1. Select the Sauté function on the Instant Pot and melt the

butter. Add the scallions, ground chicken, and nutmeg, sautéing for about 4 minutes.
2. Add coconut flour and salt, then continue to cook for an additional 10 minutes, stirring occasionally.
3. Scoop portions of the cooked chicken mixture onto lettuce leaves.
4. Serve immediately on plates.

Warm Millet Breakfast with Nuts and Strawberries

Serves: 8 / Prep time: 0 minutes / Cook time: 30 minutes

Ingredients:
- 2 tablespoons coconut oil or unsalted butter
- 1½ cups millet
- 2⅔ cups water
- ½ teaspoon fine sea salt
- 1 cup unsweetened almond milk or preferred non dairy milk
- 1 cup chopped toasted pecans, almonds, or peanuts
- 4 cups sliced strawberries

Instructions:
1. Set the Instant Pot to Sauté mode and melt the coconut oil or butter. Add millet, stirring for about 4 minutes until fragrant. Stir in the water and salt, ensuring the millet is fully submerged.
2. Secure the lid, set the valve to Sealing, and press Cancel to reset the program. Choose the Porridge, Pressure Cook, or Manual setting and set the cooking time to 12 minutes on High Pressure. Allow about 10 minutes for the pot to reach pressure.
3. When the cooking is complete, allow the pressure to release naturally for 10 minutes, then switch the valve to Venting to release any remaining pressure. Fluff and stir the millet with a fork.
4. Scoop the millet into bowls, adding 2 tablespoons of almond milk to each. Sprinkle with nuts and top with sliced strawberries. Serve warm.

Egg-Stuffed Bell Peppers

Serves: 2 / Prep time: 5 minutes / Cook time: 14 minutes

Ingredients:
- 2 eggs, beaten
- 1 tablespoon coconut cream
- ¼ teaspoon dried oregano
- ¼ teaspoon salt
- 1 large bell pepper, halved and deseeded
- 1 cup water

Instructions:
1. In a bowl, whisk together the eggs, coconut cream, oregano, and salt.
2. Pour the egg mixture evenly into each bell pepper half.
3. Add water to the Instant Pot and place the trivet inside. Arrange the filled pepper halves on the trivet.

4. Secure the lid and set to Manual mode. Cook on High Pressure for 14 minutes. When finished, perform a quick release.
5. Carefully open the lid and serve the stuffed peppers warm.

Gruyère and Asparagus Frittata

Serves: 6 / Prep time: 10 minutes / Cook time: 22 minutes

Ingredients:
- 6 eggs
- 6 tablespoons heavy cream
- ½ teaspoon salt
- ½ teaspoon black pepper
- 1 tablespoon butter
- 2½ ounces (71 g) asparagus, chopped
- 1 clove garlic, minced
- 1¼ cups shredded Gruyère cheese, divided
- Cooking spray
- 3 ounces (85 g) cherry tomatoes, halved
- ½ cup water

Instructions:
1. In a large mixing bowl, whisk together the eggs, heavy cream, salt, and pepper.
2. Turn the Instant Pot to Sauté mode and melt the butter. Add the chopped asparagus and garlic, cooking for about 2 minutes until fragrant but still crisp.
3. Transfer the asparagus and garlic to the egg mixture and stir in 1 cup of Gruyère cheese. Clean out the Instant Pot.
4. Lightly spray a baking pan with cooking spray and arrange the halved tomatoes in a single layer. Pour the egg mixture over the tomatoes, then sprinkle the remaining Gruyère on top. Cover the pan tightly with foil.
5. Pour water into the Instant Pot and place the trivet inside. Place the baking pan on the trivet.
6. Lock the lid, set to Manual mode, and cook on High Pressure for 20 minutes. After cooking, quickly release the pressure.
7. Remove the pan and foil, blot any excess moisture with a paper towel, and allow the frittata to cool for 5–10 minutes before serving

Breakfast Burrito Bowls

Serves: 4 / Prep time: 10 minutes / Cook time: 15 minutes

Ingredients:
- 6 eggs
- 3 tablespoons melted butter
- 1 teaspoon salt
- ¼ teaspoon pepper
- ½ pound (227 g) cooked breakfast sausage
- ½ cup shredded sharp Cheddar cheese
- ½ cup salsa
- ½ cup sour cream
- 1 avocado, cubed
- ¼ cup diced green onion

Instructions:
1. In a large bowl, whisk together the eggs, melted butter, salt, and pepper. Turn on the Instant Pot, press Sauté, and adjust to a lower heat setting.
2. Pour the egg mixture into the Instant Pot and cook for 5–7 minutes, stirring gently with a rubber spatula. Once the eggs start to set, add the cooked sausage and Cheddar cheese, continuing to cook until the eggs are fully scrambled. Press Cancel.
3. Divide the scrambled eggs into four bowls. Top each with salsa, sour cream, avocado, and green onion.

Spinach and Cheddar Frittata

Serves: 4 to 5 / Prep time: 5 minutes / Cook time: 20 minutes

Ingredients:
- 6 eggs
- 1 cup chopped spinach
- 1 cup shredded full-fat Cheddar cheese
- 1 cup shredded Monterey Jack cheese (optional)
- 2 tablespoons coconut oil
- 1 cup chopped bell peppers
- ½ teaspoon dried parsley
- ½ teaspoon dried basil
- ½ teaspoon ground turmeric
- ½ teaspoon freshly ground black pepper
- ½ teaspoon kosher salt

Instructions:
1. Pour 1 cup of filtered water into the Instant Pot's inner pot and place the trivet inside.
2. In a large bowl, combine the eggs, spinach, Cheddar, Monterey Jack (if using), coconut oil, bell peppers, parsley, basil, turmeric, black pepper, and salt, stirring well. Transfer the mixture to a greased, Instant Pot-safe baking dish.
3. Using a sling if needed, place the dish on the trivet, then cover loosely with aluminum foil. Secure the lid, set the pressure release to Sealing, and select Manual mode. Cook on High Pressure for 20 minutes.
4. Once finished, let the pressure naturally release for 10 minutes, then carefully switch to Venting to release any remaining pressure.
5. Open the lid, remove the dish, and serve the frittata warm.

Apple Cinnamon Almond Cake

Serves: 8 / Prep time: 10 minutes / Cook time: 50 minutes

Ingredients:
- 2 cups almond flour
- ½ cup Lakanto Monkfruit Sweetener Golden

- 1½ teaspoons ground cinnamon
- 1 teaspoon baking powder
- ½ teaspoon fine sea salt
- ½ cup plain 2% Greek yogurt
- 2 large eggs
- ½ teaspoon pure vanilla extract
- 1 small apple, chopped into small pieces

Instructions:

1. Add 1 cup of water to the Instant Pot. Line the bottom of a 7-by-3-inch round cake pan with parchment paper, and grease the sides and parchment with butter or nonstick spray.
2. In a medium bowl, mix the almond flour, sweetener, cinnamon, baking powder, and salt. In another bowl, whisk together the yogurt, eggs, and vanilla until smooth. Combine the wet Ingredients with the dry and fold in the apple pieces. The batter will be thick.
3. Spoon the batter into the prepared pan, spreading it evenly with a spatula. Cover the pan tightly with aluminum foil. Set the pan on a silicone steam rack with handles, and lower it into the Instant Pot.
4. Secure the lid and set the valve to Sealing. Choose the Cake or Manual setting, and cook for 40 minutes on High Pressure. (It may take about 10 minutes for the pot to reach pressure.)
5. When cooking is complete, let the pressure release naturally for 10 minutes, then switch to quick release. Carefully lift the pan out using the rack handles and remove the foil.
6. Cool the cake in the pan on a rack for 5 minutes, then use a knife to loosen the edges. Invert the cake onto a rack, peel off the parchment, and let it cool for 15 minutes. Slice into eight pieces and serve.

Blackberry Almond Vanilla Cake

Serves: 8 / Prep time: 10 minutes / Cook time: 25 minutes

Ingredients:

- 1 cup almond flour
- 2 eggs
- ½ cup erythritol
- 2 teaspoons vanilla extract
- 1 cup blackberries
- 4 tablespoons melted butter
- ¼ cup heavy cream
- ½ teaspoon baking powder
- 1 cup water

Instructions:

1. In a large bowl, mix together the almond flour, eggs, erythritol, vanilla extract, blackberries, melted butter, heavy cream, and baking powder. Pour the mixture into a 7-inch round cake pan (or divide it between two 4-inch pans if needed). Cover tightly with foil.
2. Add 1 cup of water to the Instant Pot, and place the

steam rack at the bottom. Set the cake pan on the rack, secure the lid, and press the Cake button. Adjust the heat to Less and set the timer for 25 minutes.
3. Once cooking is finished, let the pressure release naturally for 15 minutes, then release any remaining pressure. Allow the cake to cool completely before serving.

Nutty "Oatmeal"

Serves: 4 / Prep time: 5 minutes / Cook time: 4 minutes

Ingredients:

- 2 tablespoons coconut oil
- 1 cup full-fat coconut milk
- 1 cup heavy whipping cream
- ½ cup macadamia nuts
- ½ cup chopped pecans
- ⅓ cup Swerve, or more to taste
- ¼ cup unsweetened coconut flakes
- 2 tablespoons chopped hazelnuts
- 2 tablespoons chia seeds, soaked
- ½ teaspoon ground cinnamon

Instructions:

1. Soak the chia seeds in 1 cup of water for 5 to 10 minutes. Select Sauté on the Instant Pot and melt the coconut oil. Add coconut milk, heavy cream, and 1 cup of water, followed by the macadamia nuts, pecans, Swerve, coconut flakes, hazelnuts, chia seeds, and cinnamon. Stir well.
2. Cancel Sauté, close the lid, and set the valve to Sealing. Select Manual, cook on High Pressure for 4 minutes, and let it cook.
3. Once cooking is done, carefully turn the valve to Venting to release the pressure.
4. Open the Instant Pot, serve, and enjoy your creamy nut-based "oatmeal."

Tropical Steel Cut Oats

Serves: 4 / Prep time: 5 minutes / Cook time: 5 minutes

Ingredients:

- 1 cup steel-cut oats
- 1 cup unsweetened almond milk
- 2 cups coconut water or water
- ¾ cup frozen chopped peaches
- ¾ cup frozen mango chunks
- 1 vanilla bean (2-inch), seeds scraped, pod reserved
- Ground cinnamon, for garnish
- ¼ cup chopped unsalted macadamia nuts

Instructions:

1. In the Instant Pot, combine the oats, almond milk, coconut water, peaches, mango, and vanilla bean seeds and pod. Stir well.
2. Close the lid, set the valve to Sealing, and cook on High Pressure for 5 minutes.

3. After cooking, allow a natural pressure release for 10 minutes, then perform a quick release for any remaining pressure.
4. Once safe to open, discard the vanilla bean pod, stir the oats, and spoon into bowls.
5. Sprinkle each serving with a dash of cinnamon and top with macadamia nuts. Enjoy warm.

Bacon Bites with Cheddar Cheese

Serves: 2 / Prep time: 15 minutes / Cook time: 3 minutes

Ingredients:
- 2 tablespoons coconut flour
- ½ cup shredded Cheddar cheese
- 2 teaspoons coconut cream
- 2 bacon slices, cooked and chopped
- ½ teaspoon dried parsley
- 1 cup water (for cooking)

Instructions:
1. In a mixing bowl, combine coconut flour, shredded Cheddar cheese, coconut cream, and dried parsley.
2. Chop the cooked bacon into small pieces and add it to the mixture, stirring everything together.
3. Add water into the Instant Pot and place the trivet at the bottom. Line the trivet with parchment paper.
4. Shape the cheese mixture into small bites and place them on the trivet.
5. Close the lid and set the Instant Pot to Manual mode with High Pressure for 3 minutes.
6. Once done, perform a quick pressure release, then allow the bites to cool before serving.

Kale & Egg Casserole

Serves: 2 / Prep time: 10 minutes / Cook time: 10 minutes

Ingredients:
- ½ cup chopped kale
- 3 eggs, beaten
- 1 tablespoon almond milk
- ¼ teaspoon ground black pepper
- 1 cup water (for cooking)

Instructions:
1. In a bowl, combine chopped kale, beaten eggs, almond milk, and ground black pepper.
2. Grease two ramekins with melted coconut oil.
3. Pour the kale and egg mixture into the ramekins, smoothing the top with a spatula if needed.
4. Pour water into the Instant Pot, insert the trivet, and place the ramekins on top.
5. Close the lid, set to Manual mode on High Pressure, and cook for 10 minutes.
6. Perform a quick pressure release, then open the lid and serve the casserole warm.

Nutty Breakfast Cereal

Serves: 4 / Prep time: 5 minutes / Cook time: 5 minutes

Ingredients:
- 2 tablespoons coconut oil
- 1 cup full-fat coconut milk
- ½ cup chopped cashews
- ½ cup heavy whipping cream
- ½ cup chopped pecans
- ⅓ cup Swerve sweetener
- ¼ cup unsweetened coconut flakes
- 2 tablespoons flax seeds
- 2 tablespoons chopped hazelnuts
- 2 tablespoons chopped macadamia nuts
- ½ teaspoon ground cinnamon
- ½ teaspoon ground nutmeg
- ½ teaspoon ground turmeric

Instructions:
1. Set the Instant Pot to Sauté mode and melt the coconut oil. Add the coconut milk to the pot.
2. Stir in the cashews, heavy whipping cream, pecans, Swerve sweetener, coconut flakes, flax seeds, hazelnuts, macadamia nuts, cinnamon, nutmeg, and turmeric. Mix well.
3. Close the lid, set the pressure release valve to Sealing, and press Cancel to stop the current program. Select Manual mode and cook for 5 minutes on High Pressure.
4. Once the cooking time is complete, allow the pressure to release naturally for about 10 minutes, then carefully switch the pressure release to Venting.
5. Open the Instant Pot, serve the cereal, and enjoy!

Green Power Avocado Bowl

Serves: 1 / Prep time: 10 minutes / Cook time: 10 minutes

Ingredients:
- 1 cup water
- 2 eggs
- 1 tablespoon coconut oil
- 1 tablespoon butter
- 1 ounce sliced almonds
- 1 cup fresh spinach, sliced
- ½ cup kale, sliced
- ½ clove garlic, minced
- ½ teaspoon salt
- ⅛ teaspoon pepper
- ½ avocado, sliced
- ⅛ teaspoon red pepper flakes

Instructions:
1. Pour water into the Instant Pot and set the steam rack inside. Place the eggs on the rack. Close the lid, and set to Manual mode for 6 minutes. After cooking, quick-release the pressure and set the eggs aside.

2. Empty the water, clean the pot, and press Sauté. Add coconut oil, butter, and almonds. Sauté for 2-3 minutes, until the butter turns golden and the almonds soften.
3. Add spinach, kale, garlic, salt, and pepper to the pot. Sauté for 4-6 minutes until the greens begin to wilt.
4. Press Cancel, then transfer the sautéed greens to a bowl.
5. Peel the eggs, slice them in half, and add to the bowl. Top with avocado slices and sprinkle red pepper flakes over everything. Serve warm.

Southwest Egg Bake

Serves: 12 / Prep time: 10 minutes / Cook time: 20 minutes

Ingredients:
- 1 cup water
- 2½ cups egg substitute
- ½ cup flour
- 1 teaspoon baking powder
- ⅛ teaspoon salt
- ⅛ teaspoon pepper
- 2 cups fat-free cottage cheese
- 1½ cups shredded low-fat sharp cheddar cheese
- ¼ cup margarine, melted
- 2 cans (4 oz each) chopped green chilies

Instructions:
1. Place the steam rack in the Instant Pot and pour in 1 cup of water.
2. Grease a round springform pan that fits inside the Instant Pot.
3. In a bowl, mix the egg substitute, flour, baking powder, salt, and pepper. The mixture will be lumpy.
4. Stir in the cottage cheese, shredded cheddar, melted margarine, and green chilies. Pour the mixture into the springform pan.
5. Set the springform pan on the steam rack, close the lid, and seal the vent. Set to Manual mode on High Pressure for 20 minutes.
6. Allow the pressure to release naturally, then carefully remove the pan and let it stand for 10 minutes before slicing and serving.

Cauliflower & Cheese Quiche

Serves: 2 / Prep time: 10 minutes / Cook time: 10 minutes

Ingredients:
- 1 cup chopped cauliflower
- ¼ cup shredded Cheddar cheese
- 5 eggs, beaten
- 1 teaspoon butter
- 1 teaspoon dried oregano
- 1 cup water (for cooking)

Instructions:
1. Grease the Instant Pot baking pan with butter.
2. Pour water into the Instant Pot.

3. Sprinkle the cauliflower with dried oregano and place it in the prepared pan, pressing down lightly.
4. Add the beaten eggs and mix with the cauliflower.
5. Top with shredded Cheddar cheese, then place the pan into the Instant Pot. Close and seal the lid.
6. Set to Manual mode on High Pressure for 10 minutes, then perform a quick pressure release.
7. Open the lid and serve the quiche warm.

Chicken Mozzarella and Tomato Flatbread

Serves: 4 to 5 / Prep time: 5 minutes / Cook time: 20 minutes

Ingredients:
- For the Crust:
- 2 eggs
- 2 tablespoons salted grass-fed butter, softened
- 1 pound ground chicken (454 g)
- 1 cup grated full-fat Parmesan cheese
- ⅓ cup blanched almond flour
For the Topping:
- 1 (14-ounce / 397-g) can fire-roasted, sugar-free tomatoes, drained
- 2 cups shredded full-fat Mozzarella cheese
- 1 cup chopped spinach
- ½ teaspoon dried basil
- ½ teaspoon crushed red pepper
- ½ teaspoon dried oregano
- ½ teaspoon dried cilantro

Instructions:
1. Pour 1 cup of filtered water into the Instant Pot and place the trivet inside. In a large bowl, combine the eggs, softened butter, ground chicken, Parmesan cheese, and almond flour. Mix thoroughly, then transfer the mixture to a greased Instant Pot-friendly dish. Cover loosely with aluminum foil. Using a sling, position the dish on top of the trivet.
2. Close the lid, set the pressure release to Sealing, and select Manual mode. Cook for 10 minutes on High Pressure.
3. While the crust is cooking, mix the basil, red pepper flakes, oregano, and cilantro in a small bowl and set aside.
4. Once the crust is done, carefully switch the pressure release to Venting. Open the lid, add the tomatoes in an even layer, followed by the shredded Mozzarella and chopped spinach. Sprinkle the herb mixture over the toppings. Loosely re-cover with aluminum foil.
5. Close the lid, set the pressure release to Sealing, and select Manual mode. Cook for another 10 minutes on High Pressure.
6. Once done, let the pressure release naturally for about 10 minutes. Then carefully switch the pressure release

7. Open the Instant Pot, serve, and enjoy your homemade pizza!

Chicken and Spinach Casserole

Serves: 5 / Prep time: 5 minutes / Cook time: 15 minutes

Ingredients:
- 1 tablespoon avocado oil
- 1 tablespoon coconut oil
- 1 tablespoon unflavored MCT oil
- 1 avocado, mashed
- ½ cup shredded full-fat Cheddar cheese
- ½ cup chopped spinach
- ½ teaspoon dried basil
- ½ teaspoon kosher salt
- ½ teaspoon freshly ground black pepper
- ¼ cup sugar-free salsa
- ¼ cup heavy whipping cream
- 1 pound ground chicken (454 g)

Instructions:
1. Pour 1 cup of filtered water into the Instant Pot and insert the trivet.
2. In a large bowl, combine avocado oil, coconut oil, MCT oil, mashed avocado, shredded Cheddar cheese, chopped spinach, basil, salt, black pepper, salsa, and heavy whipping cream. Mix until well combined.
3. Grease a dish safe for the Instant Pot and add the ground chicken in an even layer. Pour the casserole mixture over the chicken and cover the dish with aluminum foil. Using a sling, place the dish on top of the trivet.
4. Close the lid, set the pressure release to Sealing, and select Manual mode. Set the Instant Pot to cook for 15 minutes on High Pressure.
5. Once the cooking time is complete, carefully release the pressure by switching to Venting. Open the Instant Pot, serve, and enjoy your casserole!

Simple Quiche Delight

Serves: 6 / Prep time: 15 minutes / Cook time: 25 minutes

Ingredients:
- 1 cup water
- ¼ cup chopped onion
- ¼ cup chopped mushrooms (optional)
- 3 ounces reduced-fat cheddar cheese, shredded
- 2 tablespoons bacon bits, or chopped ham or sausage
- 4 eggs
- ¼ teaspoon salt
- 1½ cups fat-free milk
- ½ cup whole wheat flour
- 1 tablespoon trans-fat-free tub margarine

Instructions:
1. Add 1 cup of water to the Instant Pot and insert the steaming rack inside.
2. Spray a 6-inch round cake pan with nonstick spray.
3. Sprinkle the chopped onion, mushrooms, shredded cheese, and choice of meat in the cake pan.
4. In a medium bowl, combine the remaining Ingredients (eggs, salt, milk, flour, and margarine). Pour the egg mixture over the vegetables and meat in the pan.
5. Place the cake pan on the steaming rack inside the Instant Pot. Close the lid and ensure the vent is set to Sealing. Cook for 25 minutes on High Pressure using Manual mode.
6. Once cooked, allow the pressure to release naturally.
7. Carefully remove the cake pan using the sling and let it rest for 10 minutes before cutting and serving.

Nutty Granola Delight

Serves: 12 / Prep time: 10 minutes / Cook time: 2 minutes

Ingredients:
- 2 cups chopped raw pecans
- 1¾ cups vanilla-flavored egg white protein powder
- 1¼ cups unsalted butter, softened
- 1 cup sunflower seeds
- ½ cup chopped raw walnuts
- ½ cup slivered almonds
- ½ cup sesame seeds
- ½ cup Swerve sweetener
- 1 teaspoon ground cinnamon
- ½ teaspoon sea salt

Instructions:
1. Add all the Ingredients into the Instant Pot and stir to combine.
2. Close the lid, set to Manual mode, and cook on High Pressure for 2 minutes. Once the timer goes off, allow the pressure to release naturally for 10 minutes, then release any remaining pressure. Open the lid.
3. Stir the mixture well and transfer it onto a sheet of parchment paper to cool. It will become crispy once completely cool.
4. Serve the granola in bowls as a delicious snack or breakfast topping!

Keto Cabbage Hash Browns

Serves: 3 / Prep time: 5 minutes / Cook time: 8 minutes

Ingredients:
- 1 cup shredded white cabbage
- 3 eggs, beaten
- ½ teaspoon ground nutmeg
- ½ teaspoon salt
- ½ teaspoon onion powder
- ½ zucchini, grated
- 1 tablespoon coconut oil

Instructions:
1. In a bowl, mix the shredded cabbage, beaten eggs,

ground nutmeg, salt, onion powder, and grated zucchini. Form the mixture into medium-sized hash browns.

2. Press the Sauté button on the Instant Pot and heat the coconut oil.
3. Place the hash browns into the hot coconut oil and cook for 4 minutes on each side or until golden brown.
4. Transfer the hash browns to a plate and serve warm.

Cinnamon French Toast Bake

Serves: 8 / Prep time: 10 minutes / Cook time: 20 minutes

Ingredients:
- 3 eggs
- 2 cups low-fat milk
- 2 tablespoons maple syrup
- 15 drops liquid stevia
- 2 teaspoons vanilla extract
- 2 teaspoons ground cinnamon
- Pinch of salt
- 16 ounces whole wheat bread, cubed and left out overnight to go stale
- 1½ cups water

Instructions:
1. In a medium bowl, whisk together the eggs, milk, maple syrup, stevia, vanilla, cinnamon, and salt. Add the cubed bread and stir to combine.
2. Spray a 7-inch round baking pan with nonstick spray and pour the bread mixture into the pan.
3. Place the trivet in the bottom of the Instant Pot, pour in the water, and set the foil sling onto the trivet. Place the baking pan on top of the sling.
4. Close the lid, ensuring the vent is set to Sealing. Press the Manual button and adjust the time to 20 minutes using the "+/-" button.
5. After cooking, allow the Instant Pot to release pressure naturally for 5 minutes, then quick-release the remaining pressure.
6. Carefully remove the pan, let it cool slightly, and serve.

Chicken and Egg Breakfast Sandwich

Serves: 1 / Prep time: 5 minutes / Cook time: 15 minutes

Ingredients:
- 1 (6-ounce / 170-g) boneless, skinless chicken breast
- ¼ teaspoon salt
- ⅛ teaspoon pepper
- ¼ teaspoon garlic powder
- 2 tablespoons coconut oil, divided
- 1 egg
- 1 cup water
- ¼ avocado
- 2 tablespoons mayonnaise

- ¼ cup shredded white Cheddar
- Salt and pepper to taste

Instructions:
1. Slice the chicken breast in half lengthwise and use a meat tenderizer to pound it thin. Season with salt, pepper, and garlic powder, then set aside.
2. Add 1 tablespoon coconut oil to the Instant Pot. Press Sauté, then Adjust to the "Less" temperature. Once the oil is hot, fry the egg and set it aside. Press Cancel.
3. Add the second tablespoon of coconut oil to the Instant Pot and set the temperature to Normal. Sear the chicken for 3-4 minutes per side until golden brown.
4. Press Manual mode and set the time for 8 minutes. While the chicken cooks, mash the avocado and mix it with mayonnaise.
5. Once the timer goes off, quick-release the pressure. Remove the chicken and pat it dry. Assemble the sandwich with the chicken, fried egg, shredded cheese, and avocado mayo. Season with salt and pepper, and serve.

Cauliflower Nut Porridge

Serves: 2 / Prep time: 40 minutes / Cook time: 5 minutes

Ingredients:
- 2½ cups water, divided
- ½ cup raw cashews
- ½ cup almond slivers
- ¼ cup raw pumpkin seeds
- ¼ head cauliflower, chopped
- Sea salt to taste
- ¼ cup heavy whipping cream
For the Topping:
- ¼ cup hemp seeds
- ¼ cup chia seeds
- 1 tablespoon cinnamon

Instructions:
1. In a small bowl, combine 2 cups of water, cashews, almonds, and pumpkin seeds. Soak for 30 minutes, then drain and set aside. Reserve a few nuts and seeds for garnish.
2. Pour the remaining ½ cup of water into the Instant Pot, add the soaked nut mixture, cauliflower, and sea salt.
3. Lock the lid and select Manual mode, setting the cooking time for 5 minutes on High Pressure. Once done, allow a natural pressure release for 10 minutes, then release any remaining pressure.
4. Transfer the cauliflower and nuts mixture to a food processor. Add the heavy cream and pulse until smooth.
5. Season with a pinch of sea salt, garnish with reserved nuts, seeds, hemp seeds, chia seeds, and sprinkle with cinnamon. Serve warm.

Chapter 2 Poultry

Spinach and Feta Stuffed Chicken

Serves: 2 / Prep time: 10 minutes / Cook time: 25 minutes

Ingredients:

- ½ cup frozen spinach
- ⅓ cup crumbled feta cheese
- 1¼ teaspoons salt, divided
- 4 (6-ounce / 170-g) boneless, skinless chicken breasts, butterflied
- ¼ teaspoon pepper
- ¼ teaspoon dried oregano
- ¼ teaspoon dried parsley
- ¼ teaspoon garlic powder
- 2 tablespoons coconut oil
- 1 cup water

Instructions:

1. In a medium bowl, combine the spinach, feta cheese, and ¼ teaspoon of salt. Evenly divide the mixture and spoon it onto the chicken breasts.
2. Fold the chicken breasts back together and secure with toothpicks or butcher's string. Season with the remaining 1 teaspoon of salt, pepper, oregano, parsley, and garlic powder.
3. Set the Instant Pot to Sauté and heat the coconut oil.
4. Sear each chicken breast until golden brown, approximately 4 to 5 minutes per side.
5. Remove the chicken breasts and set aside.
6. Pour water into the Instant Pot, scraping any chicken or seasoning bits from the bottom. Place the trivet into the pot and set the chicken on top.
7. Close the lid and set to Manual mode for 15 minutes on High Pressure.
8. Once cooking is done, let the pressure release naturally for 15 minutes before venting the remaining pressure. Carefully open the lid and serve warm.

Golden Turmeric Chicken Nuggets

Serves: 5 / Prep time: 10 minutes / Cook time: 9 minutes

Ingredients:

- 8 ounces (227 g) chicken fillet
- 1 teaspoon ground turmeric
- ½ teaspoon ground coriander
- ½ cup almond flour
- 2 eggs, beaten
- ½ cup butter

Instructions:

1. Cut the chicken fillet into medium-sized pieces.
2. In a bowl, combine ground turmeric, coriander, and almond flour.
3. Dip each chicken piece in the beaten egg and coat in the almond flour mixture.
4. Melt butter in the Instant Pot on Sauté mode for 4 minutes.
5. Add the coated chicken pieces into the melted butter and cook for about 5 minutes or until golden brown.

Ground Turkey and Quinoa Stuffed Peppers

Serves: 8 / Prep time: 0 minutes / Cook time: 35 minutes

Ingredients:

- 2 tablespoons extra-virgin olive oil
- 1 yellow onion, diced
- 2 celery stalks, diced
- 2 garlic cloves, chopped
- 2 pounds 93 percent lean ground turkey
- 2 teaspoons Cajun seasoning blend (plus 1 teaspoon fine sea salt if using a salt-free blend)
- ½ teaspoon freshly ground black pepper
- ¼ teaspoon cayenne pepper
- 1 cup quinoa, rinsed
- 1 cup low-sodium chicken broth
- One 14½-ounce can fire-roasted diced tomatoes and their liquid
- 3 bell peppers (red, orange, or yellow), seeded and cut into 1-inch squares
- 1 green onion, thinly sliced
- 1½ tablespoons chopped fresh flat-leaf parsley
- Hot sauce for serving

Instructions:

1. Set the Instant Pot to Sauté mode and heat olive oil for 2 minutes. Add onion, celery, and garlic, and sauté for 4 minutes, until the onion softens.
2. Add the turkey, Cajun seasoning, black pepper, and cayenne. Sauté for about 6 minutes, breaking up the meat until fully cooked.
3. Sprinkle quinoa over the turkey mixture and pour in the chicken broth and diced tomatoes with liquid. Add bell peppers on top.
4. Close the lid and set the Pressure Release valve to Sealing. Press Cancel to reset the cooking program, then select Pressure Cook (Manual) mode and cook for 8 minutes at High Pressure.
5. Once cooking is complete, allow a natural pressure release for 15 minutes before venting the remaining pressure.
6. Open the lid and sprinkle green onion and parsley over the mixture.

7. Serve in bowls with hot sauce on the side.

Tuscan-Style Chicken Drumsticks

Serves: 4 / Prep time: 15 minutes / Cook time: 12 minutes

Ingredients:

- 4 chicken drumsticks
- 1 cup chopped spinach
- 1 teaspoon minced garlic
- 1 teaspoon ground paprika
- 1 cup heavy cream
- 1 teaspoon cayenne pepper
- 1 ounce (28 g) sun-dried tomatoes, chopped

Instructions:

1. Place all Ingredients into the Instant Pot.
2. Secure the lid and set the valve to sealing.
3. Cook on Manual (High Pressure) for 12 minutes.
4. After cooking, let the pressure release naturally for 10 minutes.
5. Serve the chicken drumsticks with sauce from the Instant Pot.

Cheesy Stuffed Cabbage Rolls

Serves: 6 to 8 / Prep time: 30 minutes / Cook time: 18 minutes

Ingredients:

- 1 to 2 heads savoy cabbage
- 1 pound ground turkey
- 1 egg
- 1 cup reduced-fat shredded cheddar cheese
- 2 tablespoons evaporated skim milk
- ¼ cup reduced-fat shredded Parmesan cheese
- ¼ cup reduced-fat shredded mozzarella cheese
- ¼ cup finely diced onion
- ¼ cup finely diced bell pepper
- ¼ cup finely diced mushrooms
- 1 teaspoon salt
- ½ teaspoon black pepper
- 1 teaspoon garlic powder
- 6 basil leaves, fresh and cut chiffonade
- 1 tablespoon fresh parsley, chopped
- 1 quart of pasta sauce

Instructions:

1. Remove the core from the cabbage heads.
2. Bring a pot of water to a boil and place one head of cabbage at a time into the water for 10 minutes.
3. After cooling, carefully remove the cabbage leaves, setting aside about 15-16 leaves.
4. Combine the ground turkey and all other Ingredients, except for the pasta sauce.
5. Place a heaping tablespoon of the meat mixture in the center of each cabbage leaf.
6. Tuck the sides in and roll tightly.
7. Add ½ cup of sauce to the bottom of the Instant Pot.

8. Layer the rolls in the pot, adding a bit of sauce between each layer and on top. (Cook in batches if necessary.)
9. Lock the lid and set the valve to Sealing. Cook on Manual High Pressure for 18 minutes, then manually release the pressure when done.

Chicken with Lentils and Butternut Squash

Serves: 4 / Prep time: 15 minutes / Cook time: 28 minutes

Ingredients

- 2 large shallots, halved and thinly sliced, divided
- 5 teaspoons extra-virgin olive oil, divided
- ½ teaspoon grated lemon zest plus 2 teaspoons juice
- 1 teaspoon table salt, divided
- 4 (5 to 7 ounces / 142 to 198 g) bone-in chicken thighs, trimmed
- ¼ teaspoon pepper
- 2 garlic cloves, minced
- 1½ teaspoons caraway seeds
- 1 teaspoon ground coriander
- 1 teaspoon ground cumin
- ½ teaspoon paprika
- ⅛ teaspoon cayenne pepper
- 2 cups chicken broth
- 1 cup French green lentils, picked over and rinsed
- 2 pounds (907 g) butternut squash, peeled, seeded, and cut into 1½-inch pieces
- 1 cup fresh parsley or cilantro leaves

Instructions

1. Combine half of the shallots, 1 tablespoon oil, lemon zest, lemon juice, and ¼ teaspoon salt in a bowl; set aside. Pat chicken dry with paper towels and season with ½ teaspoon salt and pepper.
2. Heat the remaining 2 teaspoons oil in the Instant Pot on the highest sauté setting for 5 minutes (or until smoking). Add the chicken skin-side down and cook for about 5 minutes until browned, then transfer to a plate.
3. Add the remaining shallots and ¼ teaspoon salt to the pot, cooking for 2 minutes. Stir in the garlic, caraway, coriander, cumin, paprika, and cayenne, cooking until fragrant (about 30 seconds). Stir in the broth, scraping up any browned bits, then add the lentils.
4. Nestle the chicken back into the pot, skin-side up, and add the squash on top. Lock the lid and close the pressure release valve. Select high pressure and cook for 15 minutes.
5. Turn off the Instant Pot and quick-release pressure. Open the lid carefully, and remove the chicken from the pot. Discard the skin if desired.
6. Season the lentil mixture with salt and pepper, then add the parsley to the shallots and toss. Serve the chicken with the lentil mixture, topping with the shallot-parsley salad.

Sage Chicken Thighs

Serves: 4 / Prep time: 10 minutes / Cook time: 16 minutes

Ingredients
- 1 teaspoon dried sage
- 1 teaspoon ground turmeric
- 2 teaspoons avocado oil
- 4 skinless chicken thighs
- 1 cup water
- 1 teaspoon sesame oil

Instructions:
1. Rub the chicken thighs with dried sage, ground turmeric, sesame oil, and avocado oil.
2. Pour the water into the Instant Pot and insert the steamer rack.
3. Place the chicken thighs on the rack and close the lid.
4. Cook on Manual (High Pressure) for 16 minutes.
5. Once done, quick-release the pressure and open the lid.
6. Let the chicken thighs cool for 10 minutes before serving.

Herb-Infused Thanksgiving Turkey

Serves: 8 / Prep time: 5 minutes / Cook time: 60 minutes

Ingredients
- 1 turkey breast (7 pounds), giblets removed
- 4 tablespoons softened butter
- 2 teaspoons ground sage
- 2 teaspoons garlic powder
- 2 teaspoons salt
- 2 teaspoons black pepper
- ½ onion, quartered
- 1 rib celery, cut into 3–4 pieces
- 1 cup chicken broth
- 2–3 bay leaves
- 1 teaspoon xanthan gum

Instructions
1. Pat the turkey dry with a paper towel. In a bowl, mix butter with sage, garlic powder, salt, and pepper, then rub this mixture over the top of the turkey. Place the onion and celery inside the cavity.
2. Set the trivet in the Instant Pot, add chicken broth and bay leaves to the pot.
3. Position the turkey breast on the trivet. If needed, remove the trivet for better fit; it's okay for the turkey to be close to the top.
4. Close the lid, seal the vent, and cook on High Pressure for 35 minutes.
5. Allow a natural pressure release for 20 minutes, then release any remaining pressure manually.
6. Preheat the broiler. Carefully transfer the turkey to a baking sheet and broil for 5–10 minutes until the skin is crispy.
7. To make the gravy, strain the cooking juices through a sieve, reserving 2 cups. Pour the reserved broth back into the pot, set to Sauté, and bring to a boil. Whisk in

xanthan gum until it reaches your desired thickness, adding more if needed.
8. Remove the turkey from the broiler, carve, and serve with the gravy.

Instant Pot Tomato-Braised Chicken Legs

Serves: 2 / Prep time: 10 minutes / Cook time: 35 minutes

Ingredients
- 2 chicken legs
- 1 cup chicken stock
- 2 tomatoes, chopped
- 1 teaspoon peppercorns

Instructions
1. Place all Ingredients into the Instant Pot.
2. Close the lid and set to Manual mode (High Pressure).
3. Cook for 35 minutes.
4. Once finished, perform a quick pressure release.
5. Serve the chicken legs in bowls, ladling some of the cooking stock over each.

Baked Cheesy Mushroom Chicken

Serves: 4 / Prep time: 5 minutes / Cook time: 15 minutes

Ingredients
- 1 tablespoon butter
- 2 cloves garlic, smashed
- ½ cup chopped yellow onion
- 1 pound (454 g) chicken breasts, cubed
- 10 ounces (283 g) button mushrooms, thinly sliced
- 1 cup chicken broth
- ½ teaspoon shallot powder
- ½ teaspoon turmeric powder
- ½ teaspoon dried basil
- ½ teaspoon dried sage
- ½ teaspoon cayenne pepper
- ⅓ teaspoon ground black pepper
- Kosher salt, to taste
- ½ cup heavy cream
- 1 cup shredded Colby cheese

Instructions
1. Set your Instant Pot to Sauté and melt the butter.
2. Add the garlic, onion, chicken, and mushrooms and sauté for about 4 minutes, or until the vegetables soften.
3. Add the remaining Ingredients except for the heavy cream and cheese, stirring to combine.
4. Lock the lid in place. Select the Meat/Stew mode and cook for 6 minutes at High Pressure.
5. When the timer beeps, let the pressure release naturally for 10 minutes, then release any remaining pressure. Carefully open the lid.
6. Stir in the heavy cream until heated through. Pour the mixture into a baking dish and scatter the cheese on top.
7. Bake at 400ºF (205ºC) until the cheese bubbles, about 5-7 minutes.

8. Allow to cool for 5 minutes before serving.

Classic Chicken Salad

Serves: 8 / Prep time: 5 minutes / Cook time: 12 minutes

Ingredients

- 2 pounds chicken breasts
- 1 cup vegetable broth
- 1 teaspoon granulated garlic
- 1 teaspoon onion powder
- ½ teaspoon ground black pepper
- 1 cup mayonnaise
- 2 celery stalks, chopped
- 2 tablespoons chopped fresh chives
- 1 teaspoon fresh lemon juice
- 1 teaspoon Dijon mustard
- ½ teaspoon coarse sea salt
- 2 sprigs fresh thyme
- 1 bay leaf

Instructions

1. Place chicken, broth, thyme, garlic, onion powder, bay leaf, and black pepper in the Instant Pot.
2. Secure the lid and select Poultry mode, setting it to cook for 12 minutes on High Pressure.
3. Allow a natural release for 10 minutes, then release any remaining pressure manually.
4. Remove the chicken, letting it cool slightly before slicing into strips.
5. In a salad bowl, combine the chicken with mayonnaise, celery, chives, lemon juice, mustard, and sea salt. Gently mix until evenly coated. Serve immediately.

Bacon-Wrapped Chicken Tenders

Serves: 2 / Prep time: 15 minutes / Cook time: 15 minutes

Ingredients

- 4 ounces chicken fillet
- ½ teaspoon ground paprika
- 1 teaspoon olive oil
- 1 cup water (for cooking)
- 2 bacon slices
- ¼ teaspoon salt

Instructions

1. Slice the chicken fillet into two tenders, seasoning with salt, paprika, and olive oil.
2. Wrap each tender in a slice of bacon and arrange on the steamer rack.
3. Pour water into the Instant Pot, then place the steamer rack with the chicken inside.
4. Close and seal the lid, cooking on Manual mode (High Pressure) for 15 minutes.
5. Allow a natural release for 10 minutes before removing the chicken from the pot.

Creamy Cheddar Bacon Chicken

Serves: 2 / Prep time: 5 minutes / Cook time: 15 minutes

Ingredients

- ½ pound boneless, skinless chicken breasts
- 2 ounces cream cheese, softened
- ½ cup bone broth
- ¼ cup keto-friendly ranch dressing
- ½ cup shredded Cheddar cheese
- 3 slices bacon, cooked and chopped

Instructions

1. In the Instant Pot, combine the chicken, cream cheese, bone broth, and ranch dressing.
2. Secure the lid, set to Manual mode, and cook on High Pressure for 15 minutes.
3. Perform a quick pressure release once the timer is up, then carefully open the lid.
4. Stir in the Cheddar cheese and bacon until well mixed, then serve.

African Chicken Peanut Stew

Serves: 6 / Prep time: 10 minutes / Cook time: 10 minutes

Ingredients

- 1 cup chopped onion
- 2 tablespoons minced garlic
- 1 tablespoon minced fresh ginger
- 1 teaspoon salt
- ½ teaspoon ground cumin
- ½ teaspoon ground coriander
- ½ teaspoon freshly ground black pepper
- ½ teaspoon ground cinnamon
- ⅛ teaspoon ground cloves
- 1 tablespoon sugar-free tomato paste
- 1 pound (454 g) boneless, skinless chicken breasts or thighs, cut into large chunks
- 3 to 4 cups chopped Swiss chard
- 1 cup cubed raw pumpkin
- ½ cup water
- 1 cup chunky peanut butter

Instructions

1. In the Instant Pot, stir together the onion, garlic, ginger, salt, cumin, coriander, pepper, cinnamon, cloves, and tomato paste. Add the chicken, chard, pumpkin, and water.
2. Lock the lid and select Manual, adjusting to High Pressure. Cook for 10 minutes. Once complete, let the pressure release naturally. Unlock the lid.
3. Gradually stir in the peanut butter, tasting after each addition. The sauce should be thick enough to coat the back of a spoon.
4. Serve the stew over mashed cauliflower, zucchini noodles, steamed vegetables, or with a side salad.

Chicken in White Wine Sauce

Serves: 6 / Prep time: 10 minutes / Cook time: 12 minutes

Ingredients

- 2 pounds chicken breasts, trimmed of skin and fat
- 10¾-ounce can reduced-sodium cream of mushroom soup (98% fat-free)

- 10¾-ounce can French onion soup
- 1 cup dry white wine or chicken broth

Instructions

1. Place the chicken breasts in the Instant Pot. In a bowl, mix the cream of mushroom soup, French onion soup, and wine. Pour the mixture over the chicken.
2. Secure the lid and set the vent to sealing. Cook on Manual mode (High Pressure) for 12 minutes.
3. Once done, allow the pressure to release naturally for 5 minutes, then release the remaining pressure manually.

Ground Turkey Tetrazzini

Serves: 6 / Prep time: 5 minutes / Cook time: 20 minutes

Ingredients

- 1 tablespoon extra-virgin olive oil
- 2 garlic cloves, minced
- 1 yellow onion, diced
- 8 ounces cremini or button mushrooms, sliced
- ½ teaspoon fine sea salt
- ¼ teaspoon freshly ground black pepper
- 1 pound lean ground turkey (93% lean)
- 1 teaspoon poultry seasoning
- 6 ounces whole-grain egg white pasta or whole-wheat elbow pasta
- 2 cups low-sodium chicken broth
- 1½ cups thawed frozen green peas
- 3 cups baby spinach
- 3 Laughing Cow creamy light Swiss cheese wedges or 2 tablespoons Neufchâtel cheese, softened
- ⅓ cup grated Parmesan cheese
- 1 tablespoon chopped fresh parsley

Instructions

1. Set the Instant Pot to Sauté and add olive oil and garlic, cooking until the garlic is fragrant, about 2 minutes. Add onion, mushrooms, salt, and pepper; sauté for 5 minutes until mushrooms are soft. Add ground turkey and poultry seasoning, breaking up the meat as it cooks until no pink remains, about 4 minutes.
2. Stir in the pasta, then pour in the chicken broth, pressing the pasta into the liquid.
3. Cancel Sauté, then select Pressure Cook or Manual mode and cook for 5 minutes on high pressure. The pot will take about 5 minutes to reach pressure.
4. Allow a natural pressure release for 5 minutes, then release remaining pressure. Open the lid and add peas, spinach, Laughing Cow cheese, and Parmesan. Stir, let sit for 2 minutes, and then mix again.
5. Serve hot, garnished with parsley.

Simple Cajun Chicken

Serves: 4 / Prep time: 15 minutes / Cook time: 25 minutes

Ingredients

- 1 teaspoon Cajun seasoning

- ¼ cup apple cider vinegar
- 1 pound chicken fillets
- 1 tablespoon sesame oil   • ¼ cup water

Instructions

1. Place all Ingredients into the Instant Pot and secure the lid, ensuring the vent is sealed.
2. Cook on Manual mode (High Pressure) for 25 minutes.
3. Let the pressure release naturally for 10 minutes before opening the lid.

Creamy Nutmeg Chicken

Serves: 6 / Prep time: 20 minutes / Cook time: 10 minutes

Ingredients

- 1 tablespoon canola oil
- 6 boneless chicken breast halves, trimmed of skin and visible fat
- ¼ cup chopped onion • ¼ cup minced parsley
- 2 cans (10¾ ounces each) reduced-sodium cream of mushroom soup (98% fat-free)
- ½ cup fat-free sour cream
- ½ cup fat-free milk
- 1 tablespoon ground nutmeg
- ¼ teaspoon sage   • ¼ teaspoon dried thyme
- ¼ teaspoon crushed rosemary

Instructions

1. Set the Instant Pot to Sauté and add the canola oil. Place the chicken in the pot and brown on both sides, then transfer to a plate.
2. Sauté the onion and parsley in the remaining oil until the onion is tender. Press Cancel, then return the chicken to the pot.
3. In a bowl, mix the soup, sour cream, milk, nutmeg, sage, thyme, and rosemary, then pour over the chicken.
4. Secure the lid, set to sealing, and cook on Manual mode (High Pressure) for 10 minutes.
5. Allow a natural pressure release, then open the lid and serve warm.

Cheesy Chicken and Broccoli Casserole

Serves: 4 / Prep time: 15 minutes / Cook time: 15 minutes

Ingredients

- 1 cup broccoli florets • 1½ cups Alfredo sauce
- ½ cup chopped fresh spinach
- ¼ cup whole-milk ricotta cheese
- ½ teaspoon salt   • ¼ teaspoon pepper
- 1 pound thin-sliced deli chicken
- 1 cup shredded Mozzarella cheese
- 1 cup water

Instructions

1. In a bowl, combine the broccoli, Alfredo sauce, spinach, ricotta, salt, and pepper. Divide the veggie mixture into three portions.
2. Layer the chicken at the bottom of a 7-cup glass dish,

then add a portion of the veggie mix and sprinkle with Mozzarella cheese. Repeat layering, finishing with a layer of cheese on top. Cover with aluminum foil.

3. Add water to the Instant Pot and place the trivet inside. Position the dish on the trivet.

4. Secure the lid, set to Manual mode, and cook on High Pressure for 15 minutes.

5. Perform a quick pressure release, then carefully open the lid.

6. For a golden top, broil the casserole for 3–5 minutes, if desired. Serve warm.

Tender Chicken Carnitas

Serves: 8 / Prep time: 5 minutes / Cook time: 15 minutes

Ingredients
- 3 pounds whole chicken, cut into pieces
- ⅓ cup vegetable broth
- 3 garlic cloves, pressed
- 1 tablespoon avocado oil
- 1 guajillo chili, minced
- Salt, to taste
- ½ teaspoon paprika
- ⅓ teaspoon cayenne pepper
- ½ teaspoon ground bay leaf
- ⅓ teaspoon black pepper
- 2 tablespoons fresh cilantro, chopped (for garnish)
- 1 cup crème fraîche, for serving

Instructions
1. In the Instant Pot, combine all Ingredients except for the cilantro and crème fraîche.

2. Secure the lid and set to Poultry mode, cooking for 15 minutes at High Pressure.

3. Once cooking is complete, perform a quick pressure release. Carefully remove the lid.

4. Shred the chicken with two forks, discarding any bones. Garnish with cilantro and serve with a spoonful of crème fraîche.

Chicken with Creamy Spinach and Sun-Dried Tomatoes

Serves: 4 / Prep time: 5 minutes / Cook time: 18 minutes

Ingredients
- 4 boneless, skinless chicken breasts (about 2 pounds)
- 2½ ounces sun-dried tomatoes, coarsely chopped
- ¼ cup chicken broth
- 2 tablespoons creamy balsamic dressing (no added sugar)
- 1 tablespoon whole-grain mustard
- 2 garlic cloves, minced
- 1 teaspoon salt
- 8 ounces fresh spinach
- ¼ cup sour cream
- 1 ounce cream cheese, softened

Instructions
1. Place the chicken breasts in the Instant Pot, then add the sun-dried tomatoes, chicken broth, and balsamic dressing.

2. Secure the lid and set to High Pressure for 10 minutes. After cooking, perform a quick pressure release and press Cancel.

3. Remove the chicken, cover with foil to keep warm, and set aside.

4. Select Sauté mode, then whisk in mustard, garlic, and salt. Add the spinach and cook, stirring until it wilts, about 2–3 minutes.

5. Once the spinach is wilted, mix in the sour cream and cream cheese. Stir and let the sauce simmer until it thickens slightly, about 5 minutes, stirring occasionally to prevent sticking.

6. Pour the sauce over the chicken before serving.

Simple Shredded Chicken

Serves: 4 / Prep time: 5 minutes / Cook time: 14 minutes

Ingredients
- ½ teaspoon salt
- ½ teaspoon pepper
- ½ teaspoon dried oregano
- ½ teaspoon dried basil
- ½ teaspoon garlic powder
- 2 boneless, skinless chicken breasts (6 ounces each)
- 1 tablespoon coconut oil
- 1 cup water

Instructions
1. In a small bowl, mix salt, pepper, oregano, basil, and garlic powder. Rub the seasoning evenly on both sides of each chicken breast.

2. Select Sauté mode on the Instant Pot, then heat the coconut oil until hot.

3. Sear the chicken for 3–4 minutes on each side until golden brown, then remove and set aside.

4. Add water to the pot and use a spatula to scrape any seasoning from the bottom.

5. Place a trivet in the pot and arrange the chicken on top. Secure the lid and cook on Manual mode (High Pressure) for 10 minutes.

6. Allow a natural pressure release for 5 minutes, then manually release any remaining pressure.

7. Carefully remove the chicken, shred, and serve.

Thai Yellow Curry Chicken Meatballs

Serves: 4 / Prep time: 5 minutes / Cook time: 30 minutes

Ingredients
- 1 pound lean ground chicken (95% lean)
- ⅓ cup gluten-free panko
- 1 egg white
- 1 tablespoon coconut oil
- ¾ cup water
- 1 yellow onion, cut into 1-inch pieces
- 14-ounce can light coconut milk
- 3 tablespoons yellow curry paste
- 8 ounces carrots, halved lengthwise and cut into 1-inch pieces
- 8 ounces zucchini, quartered and cut into 1-inch pieces
- 8 ounces cremini mushrooms, quartered

- Fresh Thai basil leaves, for garnish (optional)
- Fresno or jalapeño chile, thinly sliced, for garnish (optional)
- 1 lime, cut into wedges
- Cooked cauliflower rice, for serving

Instructions

1. In a bowl, combine ground chicken, panko, and egg white, mixing until well blended.
2. Select Sauté mode on the Instant Pot, add coconut oil, and heat for 2 minutes. Add the onion and sauté for 5 minutes until soft. Add ½ cup coconut milk and curry paste, stirring until fragrant, about 1 minute. Press Cancel, then add water.
3. Form meatballs using a 1½-tablespoon scoop and place them in a single layer in the pot.
4. Secure the lid, set to High Pressure, and cook for 5 minutes. Once done, perform a quick pressure release.
5. Open the lid and stir in carrots, zucchini, mushrooms, and the remaining coconut milk.
6. Set to Sauté mode, bring the curry to a simmer, and cook for 8 minutes until carrots are tender.
7. Serve hot with basil leaves, chile slices, lime wedges, and cauliflower rice, if desired.

Creamy Coconut Poblano Chicken

Serves: 4 / Prep time: 10 minutes / Cook time: 29 minutes

Ingredients

- 2 Poblano peppers, sliced
- 16 ounces chicken fillet
- ½ cup coconut cream
- ½ teaspoon chili powder
- ½ teaspoon salt
- 1 tablespoon butter

Instructions

1. Select Sauté mode on the Instant Pot and heat the butter for 3 minutes.
2. Add the sliced Poblano peppers and cook for 3 minutes, stirring occasionally.
3. Slice the chicken fillet into strips, then season with salt and chili powder.
4. Place the chicken strips in the pot with the peppers.
5. Pour in the coconut cream, then secure the lid and cook on Sauté mode for 20 minutes.

Broccoli Chicken Casserole

Serves: 4 / Prep time: 15 minutes / Cook time: 10 minutes

Ingredients

- 1 cup chopped broccoli
- 2 tablespoons cream cheese
- ½ cup heavy cream
- 1 tablespoon curry powder
- ¼ cup chicken broth
- ½ cup grated Cheddar cheese
- 6 ounces chicken fillet, cooked and chopped

Instructions

1. In the Instant Pot, combine the broccoli with curry powder.
2. Add the heavy cream and cream cheese, stirring to combine.
3. Stir in the chopped chicken.
4. Pour in the chicken broth and mix well.
5. Sprinkle the Cheddar cheese over the top. Secure the lid.
6. Set to Manual mode (High Pressure) for 10 minutes. Allow a natural pressure release for 5 minutes, then open the lid and let the dish cool for 10 minutes before serving.

Spicy Mexican Chicken with Red Salsa

Serves: 8 / Prep time: 10 minutes / Cook time: 20 minutes

Ingredients

- 2 pounds boneless, skinless chicken thighs, cut into bite-size pieces
- 1½ tablespoons ground cumin
- 1½ tablespoons chili powder
- 1 tablespoon salt
- 2 tablespoons vegetable oil
- 1 (14½-ounce) can diced tomatoes, undrained
- 1 (5-ounce) can sugar-free tomato paste
- 1 small onion, chopped
- 3 garlic cloves, minced
- 2 ounces pickled jalapeños, with juice
- ½ cup sour cream

Instructions

1. Preheat the Instant Pot on Sauté mode with high heat.
2. In a medium bowl, coat the chicken with cumin, chili powder, and salt.
3. Add oil to the pot, then add the seasoned chicken. Cook for 4 to 5 minutes.
4. Stir in the diced tomatoes, tomato paste, onion, garlic, and jalapeños.
5. Secure the lid, select Manual mode, and set to High Pressure for 15 minutes.
6. Let the pressure release naturally for 10 minutes, then quick-release the remaining pressure.
7. Shred the chicken with two forks, then serve with a dollop of sour cream.

Apple Cider Chicken with Pecans

Serves: 2 / Prep time: 10 minutes / Cook time: 15 minutes

Ingredients

- 6 ounces chicken fillet, cubed
- 2 pecans, chopped
- 1 teaspoon coconut aminos
- ½ bell pepper, chopped
- 1 tablespoon coconut oil
- ¼ cup apple cider vinegar
- ¼ cup chicken broth

Instructions

1. On Sauté mode, melt the coconut oil in the Instant Pot, then add the cubed chicken.

2. Stir in the chopped bell pepper and pecans.
3. Sauté for 10 minutes, then add the apple cider vinegar, chicken broth, and coconut aminos.
4. Continue sautéing for an additional 5 minutes, then serve.

Paprika-Spiced Chicken with Tomato

Serves: 2 / Prep time: 10 minutes / Cook time: 20 minutes

Ingredients
- 8 ounces chicken fillet, sliced
- 1 tomato, chopped
- 2 tablespoons mascarpone
- 1 teaspoon coconut oil
- 1 teaspoon ground paprika
- ½ teaspoon ground turmeric
- 1 tablespoon butter

Instructions
1. Season the chicken slices with paprika and turmeric.
2. Place the seasoned chicken in the Instant Pot.
3. Add the chopped tomato, mascarpone, coconut oil, and butter.
4. Secure the lid and cook on Sauté mode for 20 minutes, stirring every 5 minutes to prevent sticking.

Creamy Pecorino Chicken

Serves: 3 / Prep time: 10 minutes / Cook time: 15 minutes

Ingredients
- 2 ounces Pecorino cheese, grated
- 10 ounces boneless, skinless chicken breast
- 1 tablespoon butter
- ¾ cup heavy cream
- ½ teaspoon salt
- ½ teaspoon crushed red pepper

Instructions
1. Cut the chicken into cubes.
2. Set the Instant Pot to Sauté mode, add the butter, and allow it to melt.
3. Add the chicken cubes and sprinkle with salt and red pepper.
4. Pour in the heavy cream, stirring to coat the chicken.
5. Secure the lid, select Poultry mode, and set for 15 minutes.
6. Let the chicken rest in the pot for an additional 5 minutes after cooking ends.
7. Serve the chicken topped with grated Pecorino cheese, allowing it to melt slightly.

Slow-Cooked Chicken Reuben Bake

Serves: 6 / Prep time: 10 minutes / Cook time: 6 to 8 hours

Ingredients
- 4 boneless, skinless chicken breast halves
- ¼ cup water
- 1-pound bag sauerkraut, drained and rinsed
- 4–5 slices Swiss cheese

- ¾ cup fat-free Thousand Island dressing
- 2 tablespoons chopped fresh parsley

Instructions
1. Place the chicken in the Instant Pot, then add the water.
2. Layer the sauerkraut on top of the chicken, followed by the slices of Swiss cheese.
3. Pour the Thousand Island dressing over the cheese, then sprinkle with parsley.
4. Secure the lid, select the Slow Cook setting, and cook on low for 6 to 8 hours until the chicken is tender.

Garlic Herb Turkey Breast

Serves: 12 / Prep time: 10 minutes / Cook time: 30 minutes

Ingredients
- 3 tablespoons extra-virgin olive oil
- 1½ tablespoons herbes de Provence or poultry seasoning
- 2 teaspoons minced garlic
- 1 teaspoon lemon zest (from 1 small lemon)
- 1 tablespoon kosher salt
- 1½ teaspoons freshly ground black pepper
- 1 (6-pound) bone-in, skin-on whole turkey breast, rinsed and patted dry

Instructions
1. In a small bowl, mix together the olive oil, herbes de Provence, garlic, lemon zest, salt, and pepper.
2. Rub the turkey breast all over and under the skin with the olive oil mixture.
3. Pour 1 cup of water into the Instant Pot, then place a trivet or wire rack inside.
4. Place the turkey breast on the rack, skin-side up.
5. Close the lid and set the valve to sealing.
6. Cook on high pressure for 30 minutes.
7. Once cooking is complete, hit Cancel. Let the pressure release naturally for 20 minutes, then quick-release any remaining pressure.
8. Open the lid and transfer the turkey to a cutting board. Remove the skin, slice, and serve.

Lemon Herb Roasted Whole Chicken

Serves: 4 / Prep time: 5 minutes / Cook time: 30 to 32 minutes

Ingredients
- 3 teaspoons garlic powder
- 3 teaspoons salt
- 2 teaspoons dried parsley
- 2 teaspoons dried rosemary
- 1 teaspoon black pepper
- 1 (4-pound) whole chicken
- 2 tablespoons coconut oil
- 1 cup chicken broth
- 1 lemon, zested and quartered

Instructions
1. In a small bowl, combine the garlic powder, salt,

parsley, rosemary, and pepper. Rub this mixture evenly over the chicken.

2. Set the Instant Pot to Sauté mode and heat the coconut oil.
3. Brown the chicken in the pot for 5 to 7 minutes, then transfer it to a plate.
4. Pour the chicken broth into the pot, using a spatula to deglaze the bottom. Place the trivet in the pot.
5. Sprinkle the lemon zest over the chicken, place the lemon quarters inside, and place the chicken on the trivet.
6. Secure the lid, set to Meat/Stew mode, and cook on High Pressure for 25 minutes.
7. Once done, allow a natural pressure release for 10 minutes, then quick-release any remaining pressure. Open the lid carefully.
8. Shred the chicken and serve warm.

Parmesan Creamy Carbonara Chicken

Serves: 5 / Prep time: 15 minutes / Cook time: 25 minutes

Ingredients
- 1 pound boneless, skinless chicken, chopped
- 1 cup heavy cream
- 1 cup chopped spinach
- 2 ounces Parmesan cheese, grated
- 1 teaspoon ground black pepper
- 1 tablespoon coconut oil
- 2 ounces bacon, chopped

Instructions
1. Place the coconut oil and chopped chicken in the Instant Pot.
2. Sauté the chicken for about 10 minutes, stirring occasionally.
3. Add the black pepper and spinach, then sauté for another 5 minutes.
4. Pour in the heavy cream and add the Parmesan cheese. Close and seal the lid.
5. Cook on Manual mode (High Pressure) for 10 minutes. Let the pressure release naturally for 10 minutes before serving.

Traditional Chicken Cacciatore

Serves: 8 / Prep time: 25 minutes / Cook time: 3 to 9 hours

Ingredients
- 1 large onion, thinly sliced
- 3 pounds chicken pieces, skin removed and fat trimmed
- 2 (6-ounce) cans tomato paste
- 1 (4-ounce) can sliced mushrooms, drained
- 1 teaspoon salt
- ¼ cup dry white wine
- ¼ teaspoon black pepper
- 1 to 2 garlic cloves, minced
- 1 to 2 teaspoons dried oregano

- ½ teaspoon dried basil
- ½ teaspoon celery seed (optional)
- 1 bay leaf

Instructions
1. Place the sliced onion and chicken in the Instant Pot.
2. In a separate bowl, mix together the tomato paste, mushrooms, salt, wine, pepper, garlic, oregano, basil, and celery seed, if using. Pour over the chicken.
3. Secure the lid and set the vent to sealing. Cook on Slow Cook mode, low for 7 to 9 hours or high for 3 to 4 hours.

Moroccan Chicken Casablanca

Serves: 8 / Prep time: 20 minutes / Cook time: 12 minutes

Ingredients
- 2 large onions, sliced
- 1 teaspoon ground ginger
- 3 garlic cloves, minced
- 2 tablespoons canola oil, divided
- 3 pounds skinless chicken pieces
- 3 large carrots, diced
- 2 large potatoes, unpeeled and diced
- ½ teaspoon ground cumin
- ½ teaspoon salt
- ½ teaspoon black pepper
- ¼ teaspoon cinnamon
- 2 tablespoons raisins
- 1 (14½-ounce) can chopped tomatoes
- 3 small zucchini, sliced
- 1 (15-ounce) can garbanzo beans, drained
- 2 tablespoons chopped parsley

Instructions
1. Set the Instant Pot to Sauté mode, then cook the onions, ginger, and garlic with 1 tablespoon of oil for 5 minutes, stirring frequently. Remove and set aside.
2. Brown the chicken with the remaining oil, then add the reserved onion mixture along with the carrots, potatoes, cumin, salt, pepper, cinnamon, raisins, tomatoes, zucchini, and garbanzo beans.
3. Secure the lid and set to Manual mode for 12 minutes on High Pressure.
4. Once cooking is complete, allow a natural pressure release for 5 minutes, then release the remaining pressure manually.

Zesty Orange Chicken Thighs with Bell Peppers

Serves: 4 to 6 / Prep time: 15 to 20 minutes / Cook time: 7 minutes

Ingredients
- 6 boneless, skinless chicken thighs, cut into bite-sized pieces
- 2 packets crystallized True Orange flavoring

- ½ teaspoon True Orange Orange Ginger seasoning
- ½ teaspoon coconut aminos
- ¼ teaspoon Worcestershire sauce
- Olive oil or cooking spray
- 2 cups bell pepper strips (any color)
- 1 onion, chopped
- 1 tablespoon green onion, finely chopped
- 3 cloves garlic, minced or chopped
- ½ teaspoon pink salt
- ½ teaspoon black pepper
- 1 teaspoon garlic powder
- 1 teaspoon ground ginger
- ¼ to ½ teaspoon red pepper flakes
- 2 tablespoons tomato paste
- ½ cup chicken bone broth or water
- 1 tablespoon brown sugar substitute (such as Sukrin Gold)
- ½ cup Seville orange spread (e.g., Crofter's brand)

Instructions

1. In a bowl, mix the chicken with the crystallized orange flavor, orange ginger seasoning, coconut aminos, and Worcestershire sauce. Set aside.
2. Turn the Instant Pot to Sauté mode and coat the pot lightly with olive oil or cooking spray. Add the marinated chicken.
3. Sauté until the chicken is lightly browned. Add the bell peppers, onion, green onion, garlic, and seasonings. Stir to combine.
4. Add the remaining Ingredients and mix well.
5. Lock the lid and set the vent to sealing. Cook on High Pressure for 7 minutes.
6. Allow a natural pressure release for 2 minutes, then manually release any remaining pressure.

Creamy Coconut Chicken Curry

Serves: 4 to 6 / Prep time: 10 minutes / Cook time: 14 minutes

Ingredients

- 1 large onion, diced
- 6 cloves garlic, crushed
- ¼ cup coconut oil
- ½ teaspoon black pepper
- ½ teaspoon turmeric
- ½ teaspoon paprika
- ¼ teaspoon cinnamon
- ¼ teaspoon ground cloves
- ¼ teaspoon cumin
- ¼ teaspoon ground ginger
- ½ teaspoon salt
- 1 tablespoon curry powder (add more to taste)
- ½ teaspoon chili powder
- 1 (24-ounce) can low-sodium diced or crushed tomatoes
- 1 (13½-ounce) can light coconut milk (choose one

without additives)
- 4 pounds boneless, skinless chicken breasts, cut into chunks

Instructions

1. Using the Sauté function on the Instant Pot (or on the stovetop), cook the onion and garlic in coconut oil until softened, then transfer to the Instant Pot.
2. In a small bowl, combine the black pepper, turmeric, paprika, cinnamon, cloves, cumin, ginger, salt, curry powder, and chili powder. Add to the pot and stir well.
3. Add the tomatoes and coconut milk, mixing thoroughly.
4. Stir in the chicken, coating the pieces with the curry sauce.
5. Secure the lid, set the vent to sealing, and cook on Manual mode (or Pressure Cook) for 14 minutes on High Pressure.
6. Let the pressure release naturally, or quick release if needed.
7. Serve with your preferred sides and enjoy!

Thai-Inspired Coconut Chicken

Serves: 4 / Prep time: 10 minutes / Cook time: 15 minutes

Ingredients

- 1 tablespoon coconut oil
- 1 pound boneless, skinless chicken, cubed
- 2 cloves garlic, minced
- 1 shallot, peeled and chopped
- 1 teaspoon Thai chili, minced
- 1 teaspoon fresh ginger root, julienned
- ⅓ teaspoon ground cumin
- 1 tomato, peeled and chopped
- 1 cup vegetable broth
- ⅓ cup unsweetened coconut milk
- 2 tablespoons coconut aminos
- 1 teaspoon Thai curry paste
- Salt and freshly ground black pepper, to taste

Instructions

1. Set the Instant Pot to Sauté mode and melt the coconut oil. Add the chicken cubes and brown for 2 to 3 minutes, stirring frequently. Remove the chicken and set aside.
2. Add the garlic and shallot to the pot, sautéing for 2 minutes or until softened. If needed, add a splash of vegetable broth to prevent sticking.
3. Stir in the Thai chili, ginger, and cumin, and cook for 1 minute until aromatic.
4. Add the browned chicken back into the pot along with the tomato, vegetable broth, coconut milk, coconut aminos, and curry paste. Stir to blend the Ingredients.
5. Lock the lid, set the Instant Pot to Manual mode, and cook for 10 minutes on High Pressure.
6. Perform a quick pressure release when cooking is complete. Open the lid carefully, season with salt and pepper, and serve.

Chapter 3 Beef, Pork, and Lamb

Pork Taco Casserole

Serves: 6 / Prep time: 15 minutes / Cook time: 30 minutes

Ingredients

- ½ cup water
- 2 eggs
- 3 ounces Cottage cheese (room temperature)
- ¼ cup heavy cream
- 1 teaspoon taco seasoning
- 6 ounces Cotija cheese, crumbled
- ¾ pound ground pork
- ½ cup tomatoes, puréed
- 1 tablespoon taco seasoning
- 3 ounces chopped green chilies
- 6 ounces Queso Manchego cheese, shredded

Instructions

1. Pour the water into the Instant Pot and place the trivet inside.
2. In a bowl, combine the eggs, cottage cheese, heavy cream, and taco seasoning.
3. Grease a casserole dish lightly and spread the Cotija cheese over the bottom. Pour the egg mixture on top.
4. Lower the casserole dish onto the trivet in the Instant Pot.
5. Lock the lid in place. Set to Manual mode and cook on High Pressure for 20 minutes.
6. Once done, quick release the pressure and remove the lid.
7. In a skillet, brown the ground pork over medium-high heat, crumbling it as it cooks.
8. Stir in the tomato purée, taco seasoning, and green chilies. Spread this mixture over the prepared cheese crust.
9. Top with shredded Queso Manchego.
10. Lock the lid back on and set to Manual mode for 10 minutes on High Pressure.
11. Quick release the pressure once cooking is complete. Serve immediately.

Smoky Chipotle Pork Chops with Tomatoes

Serves: 4 / Prep time: 7 minutes / Cook time: 15 minutes

Ingredients

- 2 tablespoons coconut oil
- 3 chipotle chilies
- 2 tablespoons adobo sauce
- 2 teaspoons cumin
- 1 teaspoon dried thyme
- 1 teaspoon salt
- 4 boneless pork chops (5 ounces each)
- ½ medium onion, chopped
- 2 bay leaves
- 1 cup chicken broth
- ⅓ cup chopped cilantro
- ½ can (7 ounces) fire-roasted diced tomatoes

Instructions

1. Set the Instant Pot to Sauté mode and melt the coconut oil. Add the chipotle chilies, adobo sauce, cumin, thyme, and salt to a food processor and pulse into a paste. Rub this paste onto the pork chops.
2. Place the pork chops in the Instant Pot and sear them for 5 minutes on each side, until browned.
3. Press Cancel, then add the onion, bay leaves, chicken broth, tomatoes, and cilantro to the pot.
4. Lock the lid, set to Manual mode, and cook on High Pressure for 15 minutes.
5. Once done, let the pressure naturally release for 10 minutes before quick releasing the rest.
6. Serve the pork chops warm, garnished with extra cilantro.

Herbed Lamb Shank

Serves: 2 / Prep time: 15 minutes / Cook time: 35 minutes

Ingredients

- 1 teaspoon coconut flour
- 2 lamb shanks
- ¼ teaspoon onion powder
- 1 sprig rosemary
- ¼ teaspoon chili powder
- ¾ teaspoon ground ginger
- ½ cup beef broth
- ½ teaspoon avocado oil

Instructions

1. Add all Ingredients to the Instant Pot and stir well to combine.
2. Close the lid and set the Instant Pot to Manual mode, cooking on High Pressure for 35 minutes.
3. After the timer goes off, allow the pressure to release naturally for 15 minutes, then release any remaining pressure. Open the lid.
4. Discard the rosemary sprig and serve warm.

Rosemary Pork Belly

Serves: 4 / Prep time: 10 minutes / Cook time: 75 minutes

Ingredients

- 10 ounces (283 g) pork belly
- 1 teaspoon dried rosemary
- 1 teaspoon salt
- ½ teaspoon dried thyme
- 1 cup water
- ¼ teaspoon ground cinnamon

Instructions

1. Rub the pork belly with rosemary, thyme, cinnamon, and salt, then place it in the Instant Pot.
2. Add water, seal the lid, and cook on Manual mode (High Pressure) for 75 minutes.
3. Remove the pork belly from the pot and slice it into servings.

Fajita Pork Shoulder

Serves: 2 / Prep time: 5 minutes / Cook time: 45 minutes

Ingredients

- 11 ounces (312 g) pork shoulder, boneless, sliced

- 1 teaspoon fajita seasoning
- 2 tablespoons butter
- ½ cup water

Instructions

1. Sprinkle fajita seasoning over the pork and add it to the Instant Pot.
2. Add butter and cook on Sauté mode for 5 minutes.
3. Stir the pork strips, then add water.
4. Seal the lid and cook on Manual mode (High Pressure) for 40 minutes.
5. When the timer goes off, allow a natural pressure release for 10 minutes.

Beef Stuffed Kale Rolls

Serves: 4 / Prep time: 15 minutes / Cook time: 30 minutes

Ingredients

- 8 ounces (227 g) ground beef
- 1 teaspoon chives
- ¼ teaspoon cayenne pepper
- 4 kale leaves
- 1 tablespoon cream cheese
- ¼ cup heavy cream
- ½ cup chicken broth

Instructions

1. Combine the ground beef, chives, and cayenne pepper in a bowl.
2. Fill the kale leaves with the beef mixture and roll them up.
3. Place the kale rolls in the Instant Pot.
4. Add cream cheese, heavy cream, and chicken broth, then close the lid.
5. Set the Instant Pot to Manual mode and cook on High Pressure for 30 minutes.
6. Once the timer beeps, perform a quick pressure release. Open the lid and serve warm.

Corned Beef Brisket with Braised Cabbage

Serves: 8 / Prep time: 15 minutes / Cook time: 1 hour 7 minutes

Ingredients

- 3 pounds corned beef brisket
- 4 cups water
- 3 garlic cloves, minced
- 2 teaspoons yellow mustard seed
- 2 teaspoons black peppercorns
- 3 celery stalks, chopped
- ½ large white onion, chopped
- 1 green cabbage, cut into quarters

Instructions

1. Place the brisket in the Instant Pot. Pour in the water and add the garlic, mustard seed, and black peppercorns.
2. Lock the lid in place. Set to Meat/Stew mode and cook on High Pressure for 50 minutes.
3. Once cooking is done, allow the pressure to release naturally for 20 minutes, then manually release the remaining pressure. Remove the brisket and transfer to a platter.
4. Add the chopped celery, onion, and cabbage to the pot.

5. Lock the lid again. Set to Soup mode and cook on High Pressure for 12 minutes.
6. After cooking, quick release the pressure. Open the lid and return the brisket to the pot to warm for 5 minutes.
7. Slice the brisket thinly and serve it alongside the vegetables.

Herbed Pork Roast with Roasted Asparagus

Serves: 6 / Prep time: 25 minutes / Cook time: 17 minutes

Ingredients

- 1 teaspoon dried thyme
- ½ teaspoon garlic powder
- ½ teaspoon onion powder
- ½ teaspoon dried oregano
- 1 cup water
- 1½ teaspoons smoked paprika
- ½ teaspoon black pepper
- 1 teaspoon sea salt
- 2 tablespoons olive oil, divided
- 2 pounds boneless pork loin roast
- ½ medium white onion, chopped
- 2 garlic cloves, minced
- ⅔ cup chicken broth
- 2 tablespoons Worcestershire sauce
- 20 fresh asparagus spears, cut in half and woody ends removed

Instructions

1. In a small bowl, mix the thyme, garlic powder, onion powder, oregano, smoked paprika, black pepper, and sea salt. Add 1½ tablespoons of olive oil and mix until combined.
2. Rub the spice mixture onto all sides of the pork roast. Refrigerate for 30 minutes to marinate.
3. Set the Instant Pot to Sauté mode and add the remaining olive oil. Once heated, sear the pork roast for 5 minutes on each side until browned. Remove the roast and set aside.
4. Add the chopped onion and garlic to the pot and sauté for 2 minutes, until softened.
5. Pour in the chicken broth and Worcestershire sauce, then return the roast to the pot.
6. Lock the lid, select Manual mode, and cook on High Pressure for 15 minutes.
7. Allow the pressure to naturally release for 10 minutes, then quick release the rest.
8. Remove the roast, cover with foil, and set aside to rest.
9. Add water to the pot and place a trivet inside. Place the asparagus in an ovenproof bowl that fits in the Instant Pot and place it on top of the trivet.
10. Lock the lid and set to Steam mode for 2 minutes. Quick release the pressure once done.
11. Transfer the asparagus to a platter, slice the roast, and serve with the asparagus. Drizzle the broth over the meat and serve warm.

Italian Beef and Pork Rind Meatloaf

Serves: 6 / Prep time: 6 minutes / Cook time: 25 minutes

Ingredients

- 1 pound (454 g) ground beef
- 1 cup crushed pork rinds   • 1 egg
- ¼ cup grated Parmesan cheese
- ¼ cup Italian dressing
- 2 teaspoons Italian seasoning   • ½ cup water
- ½ cup unsweetened tomato purée
- 1 tablespoon chopped fresh parsley
- 1 clove garlic, minced

Instructions

1. In a large bowl, mix the ground beef, pork rinds, egg, cheese, dressing, and Italian seasoning.
2. Transfer the mixture into a baking pan and smooth the top with a spatula.
3. Place a trivet in the Instant Pot and add water. Place the pan on top of the trivet.
4. Close the lid and set to Manual mode. Cook on High Pressure for 20 minutes.
5. When the timer ends, perform a quick pressure release. Open the lid.
6. Meanwhile, combine tomato purée, parsley, and garlic in a small bowl. Preheat the broiler.
7. Remove the pan from the pot and spread the tomato mixture on top.
8. Broil for 5 minutes or until sticky. Slice and serve.

Almond Butter Beef Stew

Serves: 3 / Prep time: 10 minutes / Cook time: 60 minutes

Ingredients

- 10 ounces (283 g) beef chuck roast, chopped
- ½ cup almond butter   • ½ teaspoon cayenne pepper
- ½ teaspoon salt   • 1 teaspoon dried basil
- 1 cup water

Instructions

1. Add almond butter to the Instant Pot and start preheating on Sauté mode.
2. Mix cayenne pepper, salt, and basil together in a small bowl.
3. Sprinkle the spices over the beef and add it to the melted almond butter in the pot.
4. Close and lock the Instant Pot lid.
5. Set to Manual mode and cook on Low Pressure for 60 minutes.

Pork Meatballs with Thyme

Serves: 8 / Prep time: 15 minutes / Cook time: 16 minutes

Ingredients

- 2 cups ground pork   • 1 teaspoon dried thyme
- ½ teaspoon chili flakes
- ½ teaspoon garlic powder
- 1 tablespoon coconut oil
- ¼ teaspoon ground ginger
- 3 tablespoons almond flour   • ¼ cup water

Instructions

1. In a bowl, mix together ground pork, thyme, chili flakes, garlic powder, ground ginger, and almond flour.
2. Shape the mixture into meatballs.
3. Heat coconut oil in the Instant Pot on Sauté mode.
4. Brown the meatballs in a single layer for 3 minutes on each side.
5. Add water, then cook on High Pressure for 10 minutes.

Pork Chops Pomodoro

Serves: 6 / Prep time: 0 minutes / Cook time: 30 minutes

Ingredients

- 2 pounds boneless pork loin chops, about 5⅓ ounces each and ½ inch thick
- ¾ teaspoon fine sea salt
- ½ teaspoon freshly ground black pepper
- 2 tablespoons extra-virgin olive oil
- 2 garlic cloves, chopped
- ½ cup low-sodium chicken broth or vegetable broth
- ½ teaspoon Italian seasoning
- 1 tablespoon capers, drained
- 2 cups cherry tomatoes
- 2 tablespoons chopped fresh basil or parsley
- Spiralized zucchini noodles, cooked cauliflower "rice," or cooked whole-grain pasta for serving
- Lemon wedges for serving

Instructions

1. Pat the pork chops dry with paper towels and season with salt and pepper.
2. Heat 1 tablespoon of oil in the Instant Pot on Sauté mode for 2 minutes. Add half of the pork chops and sear for 3 minutes on each side. Remove and set aside. Repeat with remaining oil and pork chops.
3. Add garlic to the pot and sauté for 1 minute. Stir in broth, Italian seasoning, and capers, scraping up browned bits from the bottom of the pot.
4. Return pork chops to the pot, layering tomatoes on top.
5. Secure the lid and set the Pressure Release to Sealing. Set to Pressure Cook or Manual for 10 minutes on High Pressure.
6. After cooking, let the pressure release naturally for at least 10 minutes, then vent any remaining steam.
7. Open the lid and transfer the pork chops to a serving dish.
8. Spoon the tomatoes and cooking liquid over the chops. Garnish with basil and serve with zucchini noodles, cauliflower rice, or pasta, and lemon wedges on the side.

Creamy Beef Brisket

Serves: 3 / Prep time: 6 minutes / Cook time: 20 minutes

Ingredients

- ½ teaspoon salt   • ½ cup water
- 14 ounces (397 g) beef brisket, sliced into strips

- ½ cup heavy cream • ½ teaspoon ground black pepper
- 1 tablespoon avocado oil

Instructions

1. Preheat the Instant Pot on Sauté mode.
2. Once it displays "Hot," add avocado oil and heat.
3. Add the beef brisket to the pot.
4. Season with ground black pepper and salt.
5. Sauté for 5 minutes, stirring occasionally.
6. Add water and heavy cream to the pot.
7. Seal the lid and set to Manual mode.
8. Set the timer for 15 minutes (High Pressure).
9. Perform a quick pressure release once the timer ends.

Cheddar Bacon Stuffed Burgers

Serves: 4 / Prep time: 10 minutes / Cook time: 9 minutes

Ingredients

- 1 pound (454 g) ground beef
- 6 ounces (170 g) shredded Cheddar cheese
- 5 slices bacon, chopped
- 2 teaspoons Worcestershire sauce
- 1 teaspoon salt • ½ teaspoon liquid smoke
- 1 cup water • ½ teaspoon black pepper
- ½ teaspoon garlic powder

Instructions

1. In a bowl, mix the beef, cheese, bacon, Worcestershire sauce, salt, liquid smoke, pepper, and garlic powder. Handle gently to avoid overworking the meat.
2. Divide the mixture into four equal portions.
3. Shape each portion into a ball and create a crater in the center using your thumb.
4. Wrap each patty loosely in foil and place them on the trivet in the Instant Pot, overlapping if necessary.
5. Pour the water into the bottom of the pot.
6. Close the lid, seal the vent, and cook on High Pressure for 9 minutes.
7. Perform a quick pressure release, then remove the foil packets and unwrap the burgers carefully.

Beef Steak with Mushroom Cheese Sauce

Serves: 6 / Prep time: 6 minutes / Cook time: 30 minute

Ingredients

- 1 tablespoon olive oil
- 1½ pounds (680 g) beef blade steak
- 1 cup stock • 2 garlic cloves, minced
- Sea salt and black pepper, to taste
- ½ teaspoon cayenne pepper
- 1 tablespoon coconut aminos

Sauce:

- 1 tablespoon butter • 2 cups sliced Porcini mushrooms
- ½ cup sour cream • ½ cup thinly sliced onions
- 4 ounces (113 g) goat cheese, crumbled

Instructions

1. Press the Sauté button on the Instant Pot and heat the olive oil. Once sizzling, add the blade steak and cook for about 3 minutes, browning on all sides.
2. Add stock, garlic, salt, black pepper, cayenne pepper, and coconut aminos to the pot.
3. Seal the lid, select Manual mode, and set to High Pressure for 20 minutes.
4. Once the cooking is complete, perform a quick pressure release and remove the lid.
5. Take the steak out and let it cool before slicing it into strips.
6. Press Sauté again, then add butter, mushrooms, and onions. Cook for 5 minutes until fragrant.
7. Add sour cream and goat cheese, simmering for a couple more minutes until well heated.
8. Return the sliced steak to the pot, mix, and serve.

Garlic Herb Beef Roast

Serves: 6 / Prep time: 2 minutes / Cook time: 70 minutes

Ingredients

- 2 pounds (907 g) top round roast
- ½ cup beef broth • 2 teaspoons salt
- 1 teaspoon black pepper • 3 whole cloves garlic
- 1 bay leaf

Instructions

1. Add the roast, broth, salt, pepper, garlic, and bay leaf to the Instant Pot.
2. Seal the lid and set to High Pressure for 15 minutes.
3. Let the steam naturally release for 15 minutes, then perform a manual release.
4. Remove the roast from the pot and slice or shred it. Store in an airtight container in the fridge or freezer.

Bavarian Beef Stew

Serves: 8 / Prep time: 35 minutes / Cook time: 1 hour 15 minutes

Ingredients

- 1 tablespoon canola oil
- 3-pound boneless beef chuck roast, trimmed of fat
- 3 cups sliced carrots • 3 cups sliced onions
- 2 large kosher dill pickles, chopped
- 1 cup sliced celery
- ½ cup dry red wine or beef broth
- ⅓ cup German-style mustard
- 2 teaspoons coarsely ground black pepper
- 2 bay leaves • ¼ teaspoon ground cloves
- 1 cup water • ⅓ cup flour

Instructions

1. Press Sauté on the Instant Pot, then add the canola oil. Brown the roast on both sides for about 5 minutes. Press Cancel.
2. Add the carrots, onions, pickles, celery, wine or broth, mustard, pepper, bay leaves, cloves, and water to the pot.
3. Seal the lid, set the vent to Sealing, and select Manual mode. Cook on High Pressure for 1 hour 15 minutes.
4. After cooking, allow the pressure to release naturally.

5. Remove the beef and vegetables and place them on a large platter.
6. Mix 1 cup of the cooking liquid with the flour and whisk into the pot. Press Sauté again and cook the mixture until smooth and thickened.
7. Serve the stew over noodles or spaetzle.

Cheesesteak Stuffed Peppers

Serves: 4 / Prep time: 10 minutes / Cook time: 8 minutes

Ingredients

- 1 tablespoon butter
- 1 pound (454 g) shaved beef
- 4 ounces (113 g) mushrooms, chopped
- 2½ ounces (71 g) sliced onion
- 1 tablespoon Worcestershire sauce
- 1 teaspoon seasoned salt   • ¼ teaspoon salt
- ¼ teaspoon black pepper
- 4 large bell peppers (any color)
- 4 slices provolone cheese   • ½ cup water

Instructions

1. Preheat the broiler.
2. Set the Instant Pot to Sauté mode and melt the butter. Add beef, mushrooms, and onion. Sauté for 2 to 3 minutes until softened. Stir in Worcestershire sauce, seasoned salt, salt, and black pepper. Press Cancel.
3. Cut the tops off the bell peppers, remove seeds and cores. Stuff each pepper with 4¼ ounces (120 g) of the meat mixture. Rinse the pot.
4. Return the pot to the base, add water and the trivet, and place the peppers on top.
5. Close the lid, seal the vent, and cook on High Pressure for 5 minutes. Perform a quick release.
6. Remove the trivet, place the peppers on a baking sheet, and top each with a slice of provolone cheese. Broil for about 1 minute until the cheese melts.

Braised Lamb Shanks with Bell Pepper and Harissa

Serves: 4 / Prep time: 10 minutes / Cook time: 1 hour 20 minutes

Ingredients

- 4 (10- to 12-ounce/283- to 340-g) lamb shanks, trimmed
- ¾ teaspoon salt, divided
- 1 tablespoon extra-virgin olive oil
- 1 onion, chopped
- 1 red bell pepper, cut into 1-inch pieces
- ¼ cup harissa, divided
- 4 garlic cloves, minced   • 1 bay leaf
- 1 tablespoon tomato paste   • ½ cup chicken broth
- 2 tablespoons chopped fresh mint

Instructions

1. Pat the lamb shanks dry with paper towels and sprinkle with ½ teaspoon salt. Set the Instant Pot to Sauté mode and heat the oil for 5 minutes. Brown two shanks for 8 to 10 minutes, then transfer to a plate. Repeat with remaining shanks.
2. Add onion, bell pepper, and remaining ¼ teaspoon salt to the pot. Cook for 5 minutes until softened. Stir in 2 tablespoons harissa, garlic, and tomato paste, and cook for 30 seconds. Add broth and bay leaf, scraping up browned bits. Place the shanks back in the pot along with any juices.
3. Lock the lid, set the vent to sealing, and cook on High Pressure for 60 minutes.
4. Allow pressure to release naturally for 15 minutes. Perform a quick release for any remaining pressure, then open the lid.
5. Transfer the lamb shanks to a serving dish, cover with foil, and let rest.
6. Strain the braising liquid and blend with the remaining harissa until smooth. Season with salt and pepper to taste. Pour some sauce over the shanks and sprinkle with mint. Serve with extra sauce on the side.

Korean Beef with Pickled Vegetable Bowls

Serves: 6 / Prep time: 15 minutes / Cook time: 10 minutes

Ingredients:

- 1 tablespoon vegetable oil
- 5 garlic cloves, thinly sliced
- 1 tablespoon fresh ginger, julienned
- 2 dried red chiles   • 1 cup sliced onions
- 1 pound (454 g) 80% lean ground beef
- 1 tablespoon gochujang, to taste
- 1 cup fresh basil leaves, divided
- 1 tablespoon coconut aminos
- 1 teaspoon Swerve (or another sweetener)
- 2 tablespoons freshly squeezed lime juice
- 1 teaspoon salt   • ¼ cup water
- 1 teaspoon freshly ground pepper
- 1 teaspoon sesame oil

For the Pickled Vegetables:

- 1 cucumber, peeled and coarsely grated
- 1 turnip, coarsely grated
- ¼ cup white vinegar   • ½ teaspoon salt
- ½ teaspoon Swerve (or another sweetener)

Instructions:

1. Select Sauté mode on the Instant Pot. Heat the vegetable oil until shimmering.
2. Add the garlic, ginger, and chiles, and sauté for 1 minute.
3. Stir in the onions and sauté for another minute.
4. Add the ground beef and cook for about 4 minutes.
5. Stir in gochujang, ½ cup basil, coconut aminos, sweetener, lime juice, salt, pepper, water, and sesame oil.
6. Lock the lid and select Manual mode. Set the timer to 4

minutes on High Pressure.

7. Once cooking is complete, let the pressure release naturally for 5 minutes, then manually release any remaining pressure. Unlock the lid and stir in the remaining basil.

8. While the beef is cooking, combine the cucumber and turnip with vinegar, salt, and sweetener in a medium bowl for the pickled vegetables.

9. To serve, divide the basil beef into bowls and top with the pickled vegetables.

Aromatic Pork Steak Curry

Serves: 6 / Prep time: 15 minutes / Cook time: 8 minutes

Ingredients

- ½ teaspoon mustard seeds
- 1 teaspoon fennel seeds
- 1 teaspoon cumin seeds
- 2 chili peppers, minced
- ½ teaspoon ground bay leaf
- 1 teaspoon mixed peppercorns
- 1 tablespoon sesame oil
- 1½ pounds (680 g) pork steak, sliced
- 2 cloves garlic, minced
- 2 tablespoons scallions, chopped
- 1 teaspoon fresh ginger, grated
- 1 teaspoon curry powder
- 1 cup chicken broth
- 2 tablespoons balsamic vinegar
- 3 tablespoons coconut cream
- ¼ teaspoon red pepper flakes
- Sea salt, to taste
- ¼ teaspoon black pepper

Instructions

1. In a skillet over medium-high heat, roast mustard seeds, fennel seeds, cumin seeds, chili peppers, bay leaf, and peppercorns for 1 to 2 minutes until aromatic.

2. Set the Instant Pot to Sauté mode and heat sesame oil until sizzling. Brown the pork steak for 5 minutes.

3. Add the roasted seasonings along with garlic, scallions, ginger, curry powder, broth, balsamic vinegar, coconut cream, red pepper flakes, sea salt, and black pepper. Stir to combine.

4. Lock the lid, set to Manual mode, and cook on High Pressure for 8 minutes.

5. Once cooking is complete, perform a quick release and carefully open the lid. Serve the curry immediately.

Beef Clod Vindaloo

Serves: 2 / Prep time: 15 minutes / Cook time: 15 minutes

Ingredients

- ½ Serrano pepper, chopped
- ¼ teaspoon cumin seeds
- ¼ teaspoon minced ginger
- ¼ teaspoon cayenne pepper
- ¼ teaspoon paprika
- ¼ teaspoon salt
- 1 cup water
- 9 ounces (255 g) beef clod, chopped

Instructions

1. In a food processor, blend Serrano pepper, cumin seeds, ginger, cayenne pepper, salt, paprika, and water until smooth.

2. Transfer the mixture to a bowl and coat the chopped beef clod.

3. Add the beef and mixture to the Instant Pot and seal the lid.

4. Set to Manual mode and cook on High Pressure for 15 minutes.

5. After the timer ends, allow for a natural pressure release for 10 minutes, then perform a quick release.

6. Open the lid and serve the vindaloo immediately.

Pork Butt Roast

Serves 6 to 8 / Prep time: 10 minutes / Cook time: 9 minutes

Ingredients

- 3 to 4 pounds pork butt roast
- 2 to 3 tablespoons of your favorite rub
- 2 cups water

Instructions

1. Place the pork butt roast into the Instant Pot.

2. Rub the roast with your seasoning of choice and add the water carefully so as not to wash off the rub.

3. Secure the lid, set the vent to sealing, and cook on Manual mode for 9 minutes.

4. Let the pressure release naturally.

Ginger Beef Flank Steak

Serves: 2 / Prep time: 8 minutes / Cook time: 13 minutes

Ingredients

- 14 ounces (397 g) beef flank steak, sliced
- 1 tablespoon almond flour
- ½ teaspoon minced ginger
- 1 ounce (28 g) scallions, sliced
- 1 tablespoon coconut oil
- ¾ cup water

Instructions

1. Toss the beef slices with almond flour and shake off any excess.

2. Set the Instant Pot to Sauté mode and heat the coconut oil.

3. Add the beef to the pot and cook for 3 minutes, stirring occasionally.

4. Add the minced ginger and stir well.

5. Pour in the water, lock the lid, and set to Manual mode on High Pressure for 10 minutes.

6. Once the cooking time is up, perform a quick release.

7. Top the cooked beef with sliced scallions and serve immediately.

Mexican Lasagna with 5 Ingredients

Serves: 4 / Prep time: 15 minutes / Cook time: 15 minutes

Ingredients:
- Nonstick cooking spray
- ½ can (15 ounces) light red kidney beans, rinsed and drained
- 4 (6-inch) gluten-free corn tortillas
- 1½ cups cooked shredded beef, pork, or chicken
- 1⅓ cups salsa
- 1⅓ cups shredded Mexican cheese blend

Instructions:
1. Spray a 6-inch springform pan with cooking spray and wrap the bottom in foil.
2. Mash the kidney beans with a fork in a medium bowl.
3. Place 1 tortilla at the bottom of the pan. Add a layer of ⅓ of the beans, ½ cup of meat, ⅓ cup salsa, and ⅓ cup cheese. Press down. Repeat the layers two more times. Top with the remaining tortilla, press down, and cover with the remaining salsa and cheese. No beans or meat are added on top.
4. Spray a large piece of foil with nonstick spray and line the pan with it, sprayed-side down.
5. Pour 1 cup of water into the electric pressure cooker.
6. Place the pan on the wire rack and carefully lower it into the pot. Lock the lid and seal the vent.
7. Cook on high pressure for 15 minutes.
8. Once cooking is complete, press Cancel. Let the pressure naturally release for 10 minutes, then quick-release the remaining pressure.
9. When the pin drops, unlock the lid.
10. Use the wire rack handles to carefully lift the pan from the pot. Let the lasagna rest for 5 minutes. Remove the ring.
11. Slice into quarters and serve.

Bone Broth Braised Brisket with Tomatoes

Serves 4 to 5 / Prep time: 5 minutes / Cook time: 75 minutes

Ingredients:
- 2 tablespoons coconut oil
- ½ teaspoon garlic salt
- ½ teaspoon crushed red pepper
- ½ teaspoon dried basil
- ½ teaspoon kosher salt
- ½ teaspoon freshly ground black pepper
- 1 (14-ounce / 397-g) can sugar-free diced tomatoes
- 1 cup grass-fed bone broth
- 1 pound (454 g) beef brisket, chopped

Instructions:
1. Set the Instant Pot to Sauté and melt the coconut oil. In a bowl, combine the garlic salt, red pepper, basil, kosher salt, black pepper, and diced tomatoes.
2. Pour the bone broth into the Instant Pot, then add the brisket and top with the pre-mixed tomato sauce. Close the lid and set the pressure release to Sealing. Cancel the current program and select Manual. Cook on High Pressure for 75 minutes.
3. Once done, release the pressure naturally and carefully switch the valve to Venting. Open the lid and serve, adding any leftover sauce over the brisket.

Easy Steak Tacos

Serves: 6 / Prep time: 5 minutes / Cook time: 10 minutes

Ingredients:
- 1 tablespoon olive oil
- 8 ounces sirloin steak
- 2 tablespoons steak seasoning
- 1 teaspoon Worcestershire sauce
- ½ red onion, halved and sliced
- 6 corn tortillas
- ¼ cup diced tomatoes
- ¾ cup reduced-fat Mexican cheese
- 2 tablespoons low-fat sour cream
- 6 tablespoons fresh salsa
- ¼ cup fresh cilantro, chopped

Instructions:
1. Turn on the Instant Pot to Sauté mode. Once heated, add olive oil to the pot.
2. Season the steak with steak seasoning.
3. Place the steak in the pot with Worcestershire sauce.
4. Sear each side for 2–3 minutes until browned.
5. Remove the steak, slice it thinly.
6. Add the onion to the pot and cook until soft.
7. Remove the onion, then warm the tortillas.
8. Assemble the tacos by adding the steak, onion, tomatoes, cheese, sour cream, salsa, and cilantro.

Chili-Spiced Pork Loin

Serves: 2 / Prep time: 10 minutes / Cook time: 20 minutes

Ingredients:
- 10 ounces (283 g) pork loin
- ¼ cup water
- 1 teaspoon chili paste
- ½ teaspoon ground black pepper
- ½ teaspoon salt

Instructions:
1. Cut the pork loin into medium pieces.
2. Sprinkle with salt and ground black pepper.
3. Coat the pork with chili paste.
4. Mix the meat thoroughly with your hands.
5. Add water to the Instant Pot, then add the pork mixture.
6. Secure the lid and set the Instant Pot to the Meat/Stew setting. Cook for 25 minutes.
7. Let the pork rest until warm before serving.

Eggplant and Pork Lasagna

Serves: 6 / Prep time: 20 minutes / Cook time: 30 minutes

Ingredients:

- 2 eggplants, sliced
- 1 teaspoon salt
- 10 ounces (283 g) ground pork
- 1 cup shredded Mozzarella
- 1 tablespoon unsweetened tomato purée
- 1 teaspoon butter, softened
- 1 cup chicken stock

Instructions:

1. Sprinkle salt on the eggplant slices and let them sit for 10 minutes, then pat dry with paper towels.
2. In a bowl, combine the ground pork, butter, and tomato purée.
3. Layer the eggplant slices at the bottom of the Instant Pot, followed by the ground pork mixture.
4. Top with Mozzarella and repeat with the remaining Ingredients.
5. Pour the chicken stock into the pot. Close the lid, set to Manual mode, and cook on High Pressure for 30 minutes.
6. Once the cooking time ends, allow a natural pressure release for 10 minutes, then release any remaining pressure.
7. Let the lasagna cool for 10 minutes before serving.

Cheddar Beef and Broccoli

Serves: 4 / Prep time: 5 minutes / Cook time: 10 minutes

Ingredients:

- 1 pound (454 g) 85% lean ground beef
- 1 teaspoon salt
- ½ teaspoon garlic powder
- ½ teaspoon dried parsley
- ¼ teaspoon dried oregano
- 2 tablespoons butter
- ¾ cup beef broth
- 2 cups broccoli florets
- ¼ cup heavy cream
- 1 cup shredded mild Cheddar cheese

Instructions:

1. Press the Sauté button and brown the ground beef in the Instant Pot until fully cooked. Press Cancel and sprinkle in the seasonings.
2. Add butter, beef broth, and broccoli, then close the lid.
3. Press Manual mode and set the timer for 2 minutes. Once the timer beeps, press Cancel.
4. Stir in the heavy cream and shredded Cheddar until completely melted. Serve immediately.

Cilantro Pork Meatballs

Serves: 3 / Prep time: 10 minutes / Cook time: 15 minutes

Ingredients:

- 1 cup ground pork
- 1 ounce (28 g) fresh cilantro, chopped
- 1 garlic clove, minced
- ½ teaspoon salt
- 1 teaspoon ground coriander
- 2 tablespoons butter
- 1 tablespoon coconut cream

Instructions:

1. Blend the fresh cilantro into a paste and mix with the ground pork, garlic, salt, and coriander.
2. Shape the mixture into small meatballs and gently press them with your palms.
3. Set the Instant Pot to Sauté mode and melt the butter. Add the meatballs and cook for 3 minutes on each side.
4. Add the coconut cream, close the lid, and cook on Sauté mode for another 5 minutes.
5. Once the meatballs are cooked through, serve warm.

Salisbury Steaks with Seared Cauliflower

Serves: 4 / Prep time: 5 minutes / Cook time: 30 minutes

Ingredients

Salisbury Steaks:

- 1 pound 95% lean ground beef
- ⅓ cup almond flour
- 1 large egg
- ½ teaspoon fine sea salt
- ¼ teaspoon freshly ground black pepper
- 2 tablespoons avocado oil
- 1 small yellow onion, sliced
- 1 garlic clove, chopped
- 8 ounces cremini or button mushrooms, sliced
- ½ teaspoon fine sea salt
- 2 tablespoons tomato paste
- 1½ teaspoons yellow mustard
- 1 cup low-sodium beef bone broth

Seared Cauliflower:

- 1 tablespoon olive oil
- 1 head cauliflower, cut into bite-sized florets
- 2 tablespoons chopped fresh flat-leaf parsley
- ¼ teaspoon fine sea salt
- 2 teaspoons cornstarch
- 2 teaspoons water

Instructions:

1. For the steaks: In a bowl, combine the beef, almond flour, egg, salt, and pepper. Mix with your hands until evenly combined. Shape into four oval patties, about ½ inch thick.
2. Select Sauté on the Instant Pot and heat the avocado oil. Add the patties and sear for 3 minutes on one side, then flip and cook for 2-3 minutes on the other side. Remove patties and set aside.

3. Add the onion, garlic, mushrooms, and salt to the pot and sauté for 4 minutes, until the onion is translucent and the mushrooms release their liquid. Stir in the tomato paste, mustard, and beef broth, scraping any browned bits from the bottom of the pot.
4. Return the patties to the pot and spoon some sauce over them. Lock the lid, set the Pressure Release to Sealing, and select Manual mode. Cook on High Pressure for 10 minutes.
5. After cooking, let the pressure release naturally for at least 10 minutes, then manually release any remaining pressure.
6. For the cauliflower: While the pressure releases, heat the olive oil in a large skillet over medium heat. Add the cauliflower and sauté, stirring occasionally, until lightly browned, about 8 minutes. Turn off the heat and stir in the parsley and salt.
7. Open the Instant Pot and transfer the patties to a serving plate. In a small bowl, mix the cornstarch and water. Press Cancel on the Instant Pot, then select Sauté. Stir in the cornstarch mixture and cook for about 1 minute, until the sauce thickens.
8. Spoon the sauce over the patties and serve with the seared cauliflower.

Shawarma-Style Beef with Veggie Salad Bowls

Serves: 4 / Prep time: 10 minutes / Cook time: 19 minutes

Ingredients:
- 2 teaspoons olive oil
- 1½ pounds (680 g) beef flank steak, thinly sliced
- Sea salt and freshly ground black pepper, to taste
- 1 teaspoon cayenne pepper
- ½ teaspoon ground bay leaf
- ½ teaspoon ground allspice
- ½ teaspoon cumin, divided
- ½ cup Greek yogurt
- 2 tablespoons sesame oil
- 1 tablespoon fresh lime juice
- 2 English cucumbers, chopped
- 1 cup cherry tomatoes, halved
- 1 red onion, thinly sliced
- ½ head romaine lettuce, chopped

Instructions:
1. Press the Sauté function on the Instant Pot and heat the olive oil. Cook the beef for about 4 minutes.
2. Add all seasonings and 1½ cups of water. Secure the lid.
3. Set the Instant Pot to Manual mode and cook on High Pressure for 15 minutes.
4. Once cooking is done, allow a natural pressure release, then carefully open the lid.
5. Let the beef cool completely.

6. To make the dressing, whisk together the Greek yogurt, sesame oil, and lime juice in a bowl.
7. Divide the cucumbers, tomatoes, red onion, and romaine lettuce into four bowls. Dress the salad and top with the cooled beef. Serve warm.

Chuck Roast French Dip

Serves: 6 / Prep time: 5 minutes / Cook time: 70 minutes
- 2 tablespoons avocado oil
- 2 to 2½ pounds (907 g to 1.1 kg) chuck roast
- 2 cups beef broth
- 2 tablespoons dried rosemary
- 3 cloves garlic, minced   • 1 teaspoon salt
- ½ teaspoon black pepper
- ¼ teaspoon dried thyme
- ½ onion, quartered
- 2 bay leaves

Instructions:
1. Set the pot to Sauté mode. Once hot, add the avocado oil and sear the roast on each side for about 5 minutes. Press Cancel.
2. Add the beef broth to the pot.
3. Sprinkle rosemary, garlic, salt, pepper, and thyme over the roast. Add the onion and bay leaves.
4. Close the lid, seal the vent, and cook on high pressure for 50 minutes. Let the steam naturally release for 15 minutes before manually releasing the remaining pressure.
5. Remove the roast to a plate and shred using two forks. Strain the jus through a fine-mesh sieve. Serve the roast au jus for dipping.

Beef Mozzarella Bake

Serves: 3 / Prep time: 15 minutes / Cook time: 25 minutes

Ingredients:
- 12 ounces (340 g) ground beef
- 1 tablespoon chopped chives
- 1 tablespoon chopped fresh parsley
- ½ teaspoon salt
- 1 egg, beaten
- 1 cup shredded Mozzarella cheese
- 1 cup water

Instructions:
1. In a mixing bowl, combine the ground beef, chives, parsley, salt, and egg.
2. Transfer the mixture to a large baking ramekin.
3. Top with Mozzarella cheese and cover with foil.
4. Pour water into the Instant Pot and insert the steamer rack.
5. Place the ramekin with the beef mixture on the rack, close the lid, and seal.
6. Cook on Manual mode (High Pressure) for 25 minutes.
7. Allow for natural pressure release for 10 minutes.

Chapter 4 Fish and Seafood

Bacon and Celery Clam Chowder

Serves: 2 / Prep time: 10 minutes / Cook time: 4 minutes

Ingredients:

- 5 ounces (142 g) clams
- 1 ounce (28 g) bacon, chopped
- 3 ounces (85 g) celery, chopped
- ½ cup water
- ½ cup heavy cream

Instructions:

1. Set the Instant Pot to Sauté mode and cook the bacon for 1 minute until it crisps up.
2. Add the clams, celery, water, and heavy cream, stirring to combine.
3. Close the lid and seal it.
4. Cook on Steam mode (High Pressure) for 3 minutes and perform a quick release of the pressure.
5. Serve the chowder by ladling the clams and creamy broth into bowls.

Tomato-Infused Cod Fillets

Serves: 4 / Prep time: 2 minutes / Cook time: 15 minutes

Ingredients:

- 2 tablespoons butter
- ¼ cup diced onion
- 1 clove garlic, minced
- 1 cup cherry tomatoes, halved
- ¼ cup chicken broth
- ¼ teaspoon dried thyme
- ¼ teaspoon salt
- ⅛ teaspoon pepper
- 4 (4-ounce / 113-g) cod fillets
- 1 cup water
- ¼ cup fresh chopped Italian parsley

Instructions:

1. Activate the Sauté function and melt the butter. Add the onions and sauté until soft, then add garlic and cook for another 30 seconds.
2. Stir in the cherry tomatoes, chicken broth, thyme, salt, and pepper. Cook for 5 to 7 minutes, allowing the tomatoes to soften.
3. Pour the sauce into a separate bowl, then place the cod fillets on top and cover with foil.
4. Add water to the Instant Pot and insert the trivet. Place the bowl with the cod fillets on top of the trivet.
5. Lock the lid and cook on Low Pressure for 3 minutes.
6. Once cooking is complete, perform a quick release of the pressure. Carefully open the lid and garnish with fresh parsley. Serve immediately.

Halibut Tagine with Olives and Spices

Serves: 4 / Prep time: 25 minutes / Cook time: 12 minutes

Ingredients:

- 2 tablespoons extra-virgin olive oil, plus extra for drizzling
- 1 large onion, halved and sliced ¼ inch thick
- 1 pound (454 g) carrots, peeled, halved lengthwise, and sliced ¼ inch thick
- 2 (2-inch) strips orange zest, plus 1 teaspoon grated zest
- ¾ teaspoon table salt, divided
- 2 tablespoons tomato paste
- 4 garlic cloves, minced, divided
- 1¼ teaspoons paprika
- 1 teaspoon ground cumin
- ¼ teaspoon red pepper flakes
- ¼ teaspoon saffron threads, crumbled
- 1 (8-ounce / 227-g) bottle clam juice
- 1½ pounds (680 g) skinless halibut fillets, 1½ inches thick, cut into 2-inch pieces
- ¼ cup pitted oil-cured black olives, quartered
- 2 tablespoons chopped fresh parsley
- 1 teaspoon sherry vinegar

Instructions:

1. Heat the olive oil in the Instant Pot on the highest sauté setting until shimmering. Add the onion, carrots, orange zest, and salt, cooking for 10 to 12 minutes until softened and lightly browned.
2. Stir in the tomato paste, three-quarters of the garlic, paprika, cumin, red pepper flakes, and saffron, cooking for another 30 seconds until fragrant. Pour in the clam juice and scrape up any browned bits from the pot.
3. Sprinkle the halibut fillets with the remaining salt, then nestle them into the vegetable mixture, spooning some of the cooking liquid over the fish.
4. Lock the lid in place and set to High Pressure for 0 minutes. Once pressure is reached, immediately turn off the pot and quick-release the pressure.
5. Discard the orange zest and gently stir in the olives, parsley, vinegar, grated orange zest, and remaining garlic. Taste and adjust seasoning with salt and pepper.
6. Drizzle extra olive oil over each serving before serving.

Garlic Yogurt Topped Salmon Steaks

Serves: 4 / Prep time: 2 minutes / Cook time: 4 minutes

Ingredients:

- 1 cup water
- 4 salmon steaks
- 2 tablespoons olive oil

- Coarse sea salt and ground black pepper, to taste

Garlicky Yogurt:
- 1 (8-ounce / 227-g) container full-fat Greek yogurt
- 2 cloves garlic, minced
- 2 tablespoons mayonnaise
- ⅓ teaspoon Dijon mustard

Instructions:
1. Add water to the Instant Pot and place a trivet inside.
2. Coat the salmon steaks with olive oil, then sprinkle with salt and pepper on all sides. Arrange the fillets on the trivet.
3. Lock the lid and set to High Pressure for 4 minutes.
4. Once the timer finishes, perform a quick release of the pressure and carefully remove the lid.
5. While the salmon is cooking, mix together the yogurt, garlic, mayonnaise, and Dijon mustard to make the garlicky yogurt sauce.
6. Serve the salmon steaks with the yogurt sauce on the side for dipping.

Herb-Seasoned Salmon

Serves: 2 / Prep time: 10 minutes / Cook time: 4 minutes

Ingredients:
- 10 ounces (283 g) salmon fillet
- 1 teaspoon Italian seasoning
- 1 cup water

Instructions:
1. Pour water into the Instant Pot and insert the trivet.
2. Rub the salmon fillet with Italian seasoning and wrap it tightly in aluminum foil.
3. Place the wrapped salmon on the trivet in the Instant Pot.
4. Close the lid and cook on Manual mode (High Pressure) for 4 minutes.
5. Perform a quick pressure release and carefully remove the foil.
6. Cut the salmon into servings and serve.

Lemon-Garlic Salmon with Cauliflower Mash

Serves: 4 / Prep time: 15 minutes / Cook time: 10 minutes

Ingredients:
- 2 tablespoons extra-virgin olive oil
- 4 garlic cloves, peeled and smashed
- ½ cup chicken or vegetable broth
- ¾ teaspoon table salt, divided
- 1 large head cauliflower (3 pounds / 1.4 kg), cored and cut into 2-inch florets
- 4 (6-ounce / 170-g) skinless salmon fillets, 1½ inches thick
- ½ teaspoon ras el hanout
- ½ teaspoon grated lemon zest
- 3 scallions, sliced thin
- 1 tablespoon sesame seeds, toasted

Instructions:
1. Using the highest sauté setting, heat the olive oil and garlic in the Instant Pot until fragrant and golden brown, about 3 minutes. Add broth and ¼ teaspoon salt, stirring to combine. Arrange the cauliflower in the pot.
2. Prepare a foil sling, folding a sheet of foil into 16 by 6 inches. Season the salmon fillets with ras el hanout and the remaining ½ teaspoon salt. Place the fillets, skin-side down, in the center of the sling.
3. Lower the salmon into the Instant Pot on top of the cauliflower. Lock the lid and cook on High Pressure for 2 minutes.
4. Turn off the Instant Pot and perform a quick release of the pressure. Carefully remove the lid and transfer the salmon to a plate, tenting with foil to keep warm.
5. Mash the cauliflower with a potato masher until smooth, then cook on the highest sauté setting for 3 minutes, stirring frequently. Add lemon zest and adjust seasoning with salt and pepper.
6. Serve the salmon on top of the mashed cauliflower, garnished with scallions and sesame seeds.

Mussels with Leeks and Fennel

Serves: 4 / Prep time: 20 minutes / Cook time: 6 minutes

Ingredients:
- 1 tablespoon extra-virgin olive oil, plus extra for drizzling
- 1 fennel bulb, 1 tablespoon fronds minced, stalks discarded, bulb halved, cored, and sliced thin
- 1 leek, ends trimmed, halved lengthwise, sliced 1 inch thick, and washed thoroughly
- 4 garlic cloves, minced
- 3 sprigs fresh thyme
- ¼ teaspoon red pepper flakes
- ½ cup dry white wine
- 3 pounds (1.4 kg) mussels, scrubbed and debearded

Instructions:
1. Heat the olive oil in the Instant Pot on the highest sauté setting until shimmering. Add fennel and leek, cooking for about 5 minutes until softened. Stir in garlic, thyme, and red pepper flakes, cooking until fragrant, about 30 seconds.
2. Add the wine, then add the mussels to the pot.
3. Lock the lid and set the Instant Pot to High Pressure for 0 minutes. Once the pressure is reached, immediately turn off the pot and perform a quick release of the pressure.
4. Discard the thyme sprigs and any mussels that have not opened. Transfer the mussels to serving bowls, sprinkle with fennel fronds, and drizzle with extra olive oil. Serve immediately.

Tomato Fish Soup

Serves: 4 / Prep time: 10 minutes / Cook time: 8 minutes

Ingredients:
- 2 teaspoons olive oil
- 1 yellow onion, chopped
- 1 bell pepper, sliced
- 1 celery stalk, diced

- 2 garlic cloves, minced
- 2 ripe tomatoes, crushed
- ¾ pound (340 g) haddock fillets
- 1 tablespoon sweet Hungarian paprika
- 1 teaspoon hot Hungarian paprika
- ½ teaspoon caraway seeds
- 3 cups fish stock
- 1 cup shrimp

Instructions:

1. Set the Instant Pot to Sauté and heat the olive oil. Once hot, add the onions and sauté until soft and fragrant.
2. Add the bell pepper, celery, and garlic, and sauté until soft.
3. Stir in the fish stock, crushed tomatoes, haddock, shrimp, paprika, hot paprika, and caraway seeds.
4. Lock the lid and set the Instant Pot to Manual mode, cooking for 5 minutes on High Pressure.
5. Once the timer goes off, perform a quick pressure release. Carefully open the lid.
6. Ladle the soup into serving bowls and serve hot.

Zesty Lemon Butter Mahi Mahi

Serves: 4 / Prep time: 10 minutes / Cook time: 9 minutes

Ingredients:

- 1 pound (454 g) mahi-mahi fillet
- 1 teaspoon grated lemon zest
- 1 tablespoon lemon juice
- 1 tablespoon butter, softened
- ½ teaspoon salt
- 1 cup water, for cooking

Instructions:

1. Cut the mahi-mahi fillet into 4 servings. Sprinkle the fish with lemon zest, lemon juice, salt, and rub with softened butter.
2. Place the fish fillets in a baking pan, arranging them in a single layer.
3. Pour water into the Instant Pot and insert the steamer rack.
4. Put the baking pan with the fish on the steamer rack. Secure the lid and seal.
5. Cook on Manual mode (High Pressure) for 9 minutes. Perform a quick pressure release once cooking is complete.

Mascarpone Tilapia with Nutmeg

Serves: 2 / Prep time: 10 minutes / Cook time: 20 minutes

Ingredients:

- 10 ounces (283 g) tilapia
- 1 garlic clove, diced
- 1 tablespoon olive oil
- ½ cup mascarpone
- 1 teaspoon ground nutmeg
- ½ teaspoon salt

Instructions:

1. Pour olive oil into the Instant Pot.
2. Add diced garlic and sauté for 4 minutes.
3. Add tilapia and sprinkle it with ground nutmeg. Sauté the fish for 3 minutes per side.

4. Stir in mascarpone and close the lid.
5. Sauté the tilapia for 10 minutes.

Citrus-Infused Fish and Asparagus

Serves: 4 / Prep time: 5 minutes / Cook time: 3 minutes

Ingredients:

- 2 lemons
- 2 tablespoons extra-virgin olive oil
- 4 (4-ounce / 113-g) white fish fillets, such as cod or haddock
- 1 teaspoon fine sea salt
- 1 teaspoon ground black pepper
- 1 bunch asparagus, ends trimmed
- 2 tablespoons lemon juice
- 2 cups cold water
- Fresh dill, for garnish

Instructions:

1. Grate the zest from the lemons until you have about 1 tablespoon and set aside. Slice the lemons into ⅛-inch slices.
2. Pour water into the Instant Pot. Drizzle 1 tablespoon of olive oil into each of two stackable steamer pans.
3. Season the fish fillets on all sides with lemon zest, salt, and pepper.
4. Arrange two fillets in each steamer pan and top with lemon slices and asparagus. Season the asparagus with salt and drizzle lemon juice over everything.
5. Stack the steamer pans in the Instant Pot and cover the top pan with its lid.
6. Lock the lid, select Manual mode, and set the cooking time for 3 minutes at High Pressure.
7. After cooking, allow a natural pressure release for 7 minutes, then release any remaining pressure. Carefully open the lid.
8. Lift the steamer pans from the Instant Pot.
9. Transfer the fish and asparagus to a serving plate. Garnish with lemon slices and fresh dill.
10. Serve immediately.

Lemon-Steamed Halibut

Serves: 3 / Prep time: 10 minutes / Cook time: 9 minutes

Ingredients:

- 3 halibut fillets
- ½ teaspoon white pepper
- ½ teaspoon ground coriander
- 1 tablespoon avocado oil
- 1 cup water, for cooking
- ½ lemon, sliced

Instructions:

1. Pour water into the Instant Pot and insert the steamer rack.
2. Rub the halibut fillets with white pepper, ground coriander, and avocado oil.
3. Place the fillets on the steamer rack.
4. Top the fish with lemon slices.
5. Close and seal the lid. Cook on High Pressure for 9

minutes. Perform a quick pressure release once the cooking time is complete.

Braised Striped Bass with Zucchini and Tomatoes

Serves: 4 / Prep time: 20 minutes / Cook time: 16 minutes

Ingredients:

- 2 tablespoons extra-virgin olive oil, divided, plus extra for drizzling
- 3 zucchini (8 ounces / 227 g each), halved lengthwise and sliced ¼ inch thick
- 1 onion, chopped
- ¾ teaspoon table salt, divided
- 3 garlic cloves, minced
- 1 teaspoon minced fresh oregano or ¼ teaspoon dried
- ¼ teaspoon red pepper flakes
- 1 (28-ounce / 794-g) can whole peeled tomatoes, drained with juice reserved, halved
- 1½ pounds (680 g) skinless striped bass, 1½ inches thick, cut into 2-inch pieces
- ¼ teaspoon pepper
- 2 tablespoons chopped pitted kalamata olives
- 2 tablespoons shredded fresh mint

Instructions:

1. Using the highest sauté function, heat 1 tablespoon of oil in the Instant Pot for 5 minutes or until it begins to smoke. Add zucchini and cook until tender, about 5 minutes. Transfer to a bowl and set aside.
2. Add the remaining oil, onion, and ¼ teaspoon salt to the pot. Cook using the highest sauté function for about 5 minutes until the onion softens. Stir in garlic, oregano, and red pepper flakes, cooking until fragrant, about 30 seconds. Add the tomatoes and reserved juice.
3. Season the bass with the remaining ½ teaspoon salt and pepper. Nestle the bass pieces into the tomato mixture and spoon some of the cooking liquid over them.
4. Lock the lid and set the Instant Pot to High Pressure for 0 minutes. Once the pot reaches pressure, turn it off and perform a quick release of the pressure.
5. Carefully remove the lid, allowing steam to escape.
6. Transfer the bass to a plate, tent with foil, and let it rest while you finish the vegetables. Stir the zucchini into the pot and let it sit for 5 minutes until heated through. Stir in the olives and season with salt and pepper to taste.
7. Serve the bass with the vegetables, garnishing with mint and drizzling with extra olive oil.

Crispy Tuna Spinach Patties

Serves: 4 / Prep time: 15 minutes / Cook time: 8 minutes

Ingredients:

- 10 ounces (283 g) tuna, shredded
- 1 cup spinach
- 1 egg, beaten
- 1 teaspoon ground coriander
- 2 tablespoons coconut flakes
- 1 tablespoon avocado oil

Instructions:

1. Blend the spinach in a blender until smooth.
2. Transfer the spinach to a mixing bowl and add tuna, egg, and ground coriander.
3. Stir in the coconut flakes and mix the Ingredients thoroughly.
4. Heat the avocado oil in the Instant Pot on Sauté mode for 2 minutes.
5. Shape the tuna mixture into medium-sized cakes and place them in the hot oil.
6. Cook the cakes on Sauté mode for 3 minutes on one side. Flip them and cook for an additional 3 minutes or until they are lightly browned on both sides.

Salmon with Garlicky Broccoli Rabe and White Beans

Serves: 4 / Prep time: 20 minutes / Cook time: 10 minutes

Ingredients:

- 2 tablespoons extra-virgin olive oil, plus extra for drizzling
- 4 garlic cloves, sliced thin
- ½ cup chicken or vegetable broth
- ¼ teaspoon red pepper flakes
- 1 lemon, sliced ¼ inch thick, plus lemon wedges for serving
- 4 (6-ounce / 170-g) skinless salmon fillets, 1½ inches thick
- ½ teaspoon table salt   • ¼ teaspoon pepper
- 1 pound (454 g) broccoli rabe, trimmed and cut into 1-inch pieces
- 1 (15-ounce / 425-g) can cannellini beans, rinsed

Instructions:

1. Using the highest sauté function, heat olive oil in the Instant Pot and cook garlic until fragrant and light golden brown, about 3 minutes. Remove the garlic with a slotted spoon and set aside.
2. Turn off the Instant Pot, then stir in the broth and red pepper flakes.
3. Fold a sheet of aluminum foil into a 16x6-inch sling. Arrange lemon slices across the center of the sling and place the salmon fillets, skin side down, on top.
4. Using the sling, lower the salmon into the Instant Pot. Lock the lid in place and cook on High Pressure for 3 minutes.
5. Turn off the Instant Pot and perform a quick pressure release. Carefully remove the lid.
6. Using the sling, transfer the salmon to a plate and tent with foil.
7. Stir in broccoli rabe and beans into the cooking liquid, partially cover, and cook on high sauté for 5 minutes

8. Season with salt and pepper to taste. Serve the salmon with the broccoli rabe mixture and garnish with garlic chips, extra olive oil, and lemon wedges.

Snapper in Spicy Tomato Sauce

Serves: 6 / Prep time: 5 minutes / Cook time: 5 minutes

Ingredients:

- 2 teaspoons coconut oil, melted
- 1 teaspoon celery seeds
- ½ teaspoon fresh grated ginger
- ½ teaspoon cumin seeds
- 1 yellow onion, chopped
- 2 cloves garlic, minced
- 1½ pounds (680 g) snapper fillets
- ¾ cup vegetable broth
- 1 (4-ounce / 113-g) can fire-roasted diced tomatoes
- 1 bell pepper, sliced   • 1 jalapeño pepper, minced
- Sea salt and ground black pepper, to taste
- ¼ teaspoon chili flakes • ½ teaspoon turmeric powder

Instructions:

1. Set the Instant Pot to Sauté mode and heat coconut oil. Add celery seeds, fresh ginger, and cumin seeds, sautéing until fragrant.
2. Add chopped onion and continue sautéing until softened.
3. Stir in garlic and cook for 30 seconds. Add the remaining Ingredients and stir well.
4. Lock the lid, select Manual mode, and set the cooking time to 3 minutes at Low Pressure.
5. Once the timer beeps, perform a quick pressure release and carefully remove the lid.
6. Serve the snapper warm with the spicy tomato sauce.

Creamy Shrimp Zoodle Alfredo

Serves: 4 / Prep time: 10 minutes / Cook time: 10 minutes

Ingredients:

- 10 ounces (283 g) salmon fillet (2 fillets)
- 4 ounces (113 g) Mozzarella, sliced
- 4 cherry tomatoes, sliced   • 1 teaspoon erythritol
- 1 teaspoon dried basil   • 1 tablespoon butter
- ½ teaspoon ground black pepper
- 1 tablespoon apple cider vinegar
- 1 cup water for cooking

Instructions:

1. Melt the butter using Sauté mode, then cook the shrimp, seasoning with seafood seasoning for 2 minutes.
2. Spiralize the zucchini and add it to the shrimp.
3. Add coconut cream and seal the Instant Pot. Cook on Sauté mode for 8 minutes.

Lemon-Infused Salmon with Tomatoes

Serves: 4 / Prep time: 7 minutes / Cook time: 21 minutes

Ingredients:

- 1 tablespoon unsalted butter
- 3 cloves garlic, minced
- ¼ cup lemon juice
- 1¼ cups fresh or canned diced tomatoes
- 1 tablespoon chopped fresh flat-leaf parsley, plus more for garnish
- ¼ teaspoon ground black pepper
- 4 (6-ounce / 170-g) skinless salmon fillets
- 1 teaspoon fine sea salt
- Lemon wedges, for garnish

Instructions:

1. Add butter to the Instant Pot and select Sauté mode. Once melted, add garlic and sauté for 1 minute.
2. Stir in lemon juice, tomatoes, parsley, and pepper. Let simmer for 5 minutes until the liquid reduces slightly.
3. Rinse the salmon fillets and pat dry with paper towels. Sprinkle with salt on all sides.
4. Push the sauce to one side of the pot and place the salmon on the other side. Spoon sauce over the salmon.
5. Sauté uncovered for another 15 minutes, or until the salmon easily flakes with a fork.
6. Transfer the salmon to a serving plate and serve with the sauce. Garnish with parsley and lemon wedges.

Salmon with Bok Choy

Serves: 4 / Prep time: 5 minutes / Cook time: 8 minutes

Ingredients:

- 1½ cups water
- 2 tablespoons unsalted butter
- 4 (1-inch thick) salmon fillets
- ½ teaspoon cayenne pepper
- Sea salt and freshly ground pepper, to taste
- 2 cups bok choy, sliced
- 1 cup chicken broth
- 3 cloves garlic, minced
- 1 teaspoon grated lemon zest
- ½ teaspoon dried dill weed

Instructions:

1. Pour water into the Instant Pot and insert a trivet.
2. Brush the salmon fillets with melted butter and season with cayenne pepper, salt, and black pepper.
3. Lock the lid and set the Instant Pot to Manual mode for 3 minutes at Low Pressure.
4. When the timer beeps, perform a quick pressure release and remove the lid.
5. Add bok choy, chicken broth, garlic, lemon zest, and dill to the pot.
6. Lock the lid again, set to Manual mode, and cook for 5 minutes at High Pressure.
7. Perform a quick pressure release once the timer is done.
8. Serve the poached salmon with the bok choy mixture on the side.

Cod with Olives

Serves: 2 / Prep time: 15 minutes / Cook time: 10 minutes

Ingredients:
- 8 ounces (227 g) cod fillet
- 1 teaspoon olive oil
- 1 cup water, for cooking
- ¼ cup sliced olives
- ¼ teaspoon salt

Instructions:
1. Pour water into the Instant Pot and insert the steamer rack.
2. Cut the cod fillet into two pieces and season with salt and olive oil.
3. Place the fish on foil and top with sliced olives. Wrap the fish and transfer it to the steamer rack.
4. Close the lid and seal it. Cook on Manual mode (High Pressure) for 10 minutes.
5. Allow for a natural pressure release for 5 minutes.

Flounder Meunière

Serves: 4 / Prep time: 15 minutes / Cook time: 10 minutes

Ingredients:
- 16 ounces (454 g) flounder fillet
- ½ teaspoon ground black pepper
- ½ teaspoon salt
- ½ cup almond flour
- 2 tablespoons olive oil
- 1 tablespoon lemon juice
- 1 teaspoon chopped fresh parsley

Instructions:
1. Cut the fish fillets into 4 servings and season with salt, pepper, and lemon juice.
2. Heat the Instant Pot on Sauté mode for 2 minutes, then add olive oil.
3. Coat the flounder fillets in almond flour and place them in the hot olive oil.
4. Sauté the fish fillets for 4 minutes, then flip them to the other side.
5. Cook for 3 more minutes, or until golden brown.
6. Sprinkle the cooked flounder with fresh parsley.

Lemon Pepper Tilapia with Broccoli and Carrots

Serves: 4 / Prep time: 0 minutes / Cook time: 15 minutes

Ingredients:
- 1 pound tilapia fillets
- 1 teaspoon lemon pepper seasoning
- ¼ teaspoon fine sea salt
- 2 tablespoons extra-virgin olive oil
- 2 garlic cloves, minced
- 1 small yellow onion, sliced
- ½ cup low-sodium vegetable broth
- 2 tablespoons fresh lemon juice
- 1 pound broccoli crowns, cut into bite-size florets
- 8 ounces carrots, cut into ¼-inch thick rounds

Instructions:
1. Sprinkle the tilapia fillets with lemon pepper seasoning and salt.
2. Select the Sauté setting on the Instant Pot, heat oil, and cook garlic for 2 minutes until bubbling but not browned. Add the onion and sauté for 3 more minutes.
3. Pour in the broth and lemon juice, stirring to release any browned bits from the pot. Add the tilapia fillets in a single layer and top with broccoli and carrots.
4. Secure the lid, set Pressure Release to Sealing, and press Cancel. Select Pressure Cook (or Manual) and set for 1 minute at low pressure.
5. After cooking, let the pressure release naturally for 10 minutes, then switch the Pressure Release to Venting to release any remaining steam.
6. Open the pot and use a fish spatula to transfer the vegetables and fillets to plates. Serve immediately.

Rosemary Catfish

Serves: 4 / Prep time: 10 minutes / Cook time: 20 minutes

Ingredients:
- 16 ounces (454 g) catfish fillet
- 1 tablespoon dried rosemary
- 1 teaspoon garlic powder
- 1 tablespoon avocado oil
- 1 cup water, for cooking
- 1 teaspoon salt

Instructions:
1. Cut the catfish fillet into 4 steaks.
2. Sprinkle them with dried rosemary, garlic powder, avocado oil, and salt.
3. Place the fish steaks in a baking mold in a single layer.
4. Pour water into the Instant Pot and insert the steamer rack.
5. Place the baking mold with fish on the rack.
6. Close and seal the lid, then cook on Manual (High Pressure) for 20 minutes.
7. Perform a quick pressure release.

Cheesy Mackerel and Broccoli Bake

Serves: 5 / Prep time: 15 minutes / Cook time: 15 minutes

Ingredients:
- 1 cup shredded broccoli
- 10 ounces (283 g) mackerel, chopped
- ½ cup shredded Cheddar cheese
- 1 cup coconut milk
- 1 teaspoon salt
- 1 teaspoon ground cumin

Instructions:
1. Season the chopped mackerel with ground cumin and salt, then place it in the Instant Pot.
2. Top with shredded broccoli and Cheddar cheese.
3. Pour coconut milk over the mixture. Seal the lid.
4. Set the Instant Pot to Manual mode (High Pressure) and cook for 15 minutes.
5. After cooking, let the pressure release naturally for 10 minutes before opening the lid.

Steamed Lobster Tails with Thyme

Serves: 4 / Prep time: 10 minutes / Cook time: 4 minutes

Ingredients:

- 4 lobster tails
- 1 cup water
- 1 tablespoon butter, softened
- 1 teaspoon dried thyme

Instructions:

1. Pour water into the Instant Pot and insert the steamer rack.
2. Place the lobster tails on the rack and close the lid.
3. Cook on Manual mode (High Pressure) for 4 minutes.
4. Perform a quick pressure release.
5. Mix the butter with dried thyme, then peel the lobster tails and rub them with the thyme butter.

Asian Cod with Brown Rice, Asparagus, and Mushrooms

Serves: 2 / Prep time: 5 minutes / Cook time: 25 minutes

Ingredients:

- ¾ cup Minute brand brown rice
- ½ cup water
- Two 5-ounce skinless cod fillets
- 1 tablespoon soy sauce or tamari
- 1 tablespoon fresh lemon juice
- ½ teaspoon peeled and grated fresh ginger
- 1 tablespoon extra-virgin olive oil or 1 tablespoon unsalted butter, cut into 8 pieces
- 2 green onions, white and green parts, thinly sliced
- 12 ounces asparagus, trimmed
- 4 ounces shiitake mushrooms, stems removed and sliced
- ⅛ teaspoon fine sea salt
- ⅛ teaspoon freshly ground black pepper
- Lemon wedges for serving

Instructions:

1. Pour 1 cup of water into the Instant Pot and prepare two-tier stackable stainless-steel containers.
2. In one container, combine the rice and ½ cup water, shaking it to spread the rice evenly. Place the fish fillets on top. Mix the soy sauce, lemon juice, and ginger, then pour it over the fillets. Drizzle 1 teaspoon olive oil or top with butter pieces, then sprinkle the green onions on and around the fish.
3. In the second container, arrange the asparagus in an even layer and place the mushrooms on the sides. Drizzle with the remaining olive oil or place butter pieces on top. Sprinkle with salt and pepper.
4. Place the container with rice and fish on the bottom and the vegetable container on top. Cover and latch the containers together. Lower them into the Instant Pot.
5. Secure the lid, set the Pressure Release to Sealing, and select Pressure Cook or Manual for 15 minutes at high pressure.

6. After the cooking program ends, allow for a natural pressure release for 5 minutes, then move the Pressure Release to Venting to release any remaining steam.
7. Carefully lift out the stacked containers using heat-resistant mitts, unstack them, and open the containers.
8. Serve the vegetables, rice, and fish immediately, with lemon wedges on the side.

Pan-Seared Cod with Herbed Tabbouleh

Serves: 4 / Prep time: 10 minutes / Cook time: 6 minutes

Ingredients:

- 1 cup medium-grind bulgur, rinsed
- 1 teaspoon table salt, divided
- 1 lemon, sliced ¼ inch thick, plus 2 tablespoons juice
- 4 (6-ounce / 170-g) skinless cod fillets, 1½ inches thick
- 3 tablespoons extra-virgin olive oil, divided, plus extra for drizzling
- ¼ teaspoon pepper
- 1 small shallot, minced
- 10 ounces (283 g) cherry tomatoes, halved
- 1 cup chopped fresh parsley
- ½ cup chopped fresh mint

Instructions:

1. Add the trivet to the Instant Pot and pour in ½ cup water. Fold a sheet of aluminum foil into a 16 by 6-inch sling and place a 1½-quart soufflé dish on top. Add 1 cup water, bulgur, and ½ teaspoon salt into the dish. Lower the dish into the pot using the sling.
2. Lock the lid, set to high pressure, and cook for 3 minutes. Once done, quick-release the pressure and remove the lid. Transfer the dish to a wire rack and let it cool.
3. Remove the trivet and lay lemon slices in two rows across the sling. Brush the cod fillets with 1 tablespoon of olive oil, then season with the remaining salt and pepper. Arrange the fillets skin-side down on top of the lemon. Lower the cod into the Instant Pot using the sling.
4. Lock the lid and cook on high pressure for 3 minutes.
5. In a bowl, whisk together the remaining oil, lemon juice, and shallot. Add the bulgur, tomatoes, parsley, and mint, tossing gently to combine.
6. Once cooking is done, quick-release the pressure and remove the lid. Carefully transfer the cod to a plate and remove the lemon slices. Serve the cod on top of the salad, drizzling with additional olive oil.

Louisiana Shrimp Gumbo

Serves: 6 / Prep time: 10 minutes / Cook time: 4 minutes

Ingredients:

- 1 pound (454 g) shrimp
- ¼ cup chopped celery stalk
- 1 chili pepper, chopped
- ¼ cup chopped okra

- 1 tablespoon coconut oil
- 2 cups chicken broth
- 1 teaspoon sugar-free tomato paste

Instructions:
1. Add all Ingredients to the Instant Pot and stir until a light red color forms.
2. Close and seal the lid.
3. Cook on Manual mode (High Pressure) for 4 minutes.
4. Once the cooking time is finished, allow the natural pressure release for 10 minutes.

Shrimp Louie Salad with Thousand Island Dressing

Serves: 4 / Prep time: 5 minutes / Cook time: 20 minutes

Ingredients:
- 2 cups water
- 1½ teaspoons fine sea salt
- 1 pound medium shrimp, peeled and deveined
- 4 large eggs
- ¼ cup mayonnaise
- Thousand Island Dressing:
- ¼ cup no-sugar-added ketchup
- 1 tablespoon fresh lemon juice
- 1 teaspoon Worcestershire sauce
- ⅛ teaspoon cayenne pepper
- Freshly ground black pepper
- 2 green onions, white and green parts, thinly sliced
- 2 hearts romaine lettuce or 1 head iceberg lettuce, shredded
- 1 English cucumber, sliced
- 8 radishes, sliced
- 1 cup cherry tomatoes, sliced
- 1 large avocado, pitted, peeled, and sliced

Instructions:
1. Combine water and salt in the Instant Pot, stirring to dissolve the salt.
2. Secure the lid, set the Pressure Release to Sealing, and select the Steam setting for 0 minutes at low pressure. (The pot will take about 10 minutes to come up to pressure.)
3. Meanwhile, prepare an ice bath.
4. Once the cooking program ends, perform a quick release by moving the Pressure Release to Venting. Stir in the shrimp, ensuring they are fully submerged. Cover the pot and leave the shrimp on the Keep Warm setting for 2 minutes to gently cook.
5. Remove the shrimp and transfer them to the ice bath to cool for 5 minutes. Drain them and set aside in the refrigerator.
6. Rinse the inner pot and return it to the housing. Add 1 cup of water and insert the metal steam rack. Place the eggs on top.
7. Secure the lid, set the Pressure Release to Sealing, and select the Egg, Pressure Cook, or Manual setting for 5 minutes at high pressure.
8. While the eggs cook, prepare another ice bath.
9. When the cooking program ends, let the pressure release naturally for 5 minutes, then perform a quick release. Transfer the eggs to the ice bath to cool for 5 minutes, then drain.
10. For the dressing: Stir together the ketchup, mayonnaise, lemon juice, Worcestershire sauce, cayenne pepper, ¼ teaspoon black pepper, and green onions.
11. Arrange the lettuce, cucumber, radishes, tomatoes, and avocado on plates. Top with shrimp and quartered eggs.
12. Spoon the dressing over the salads and top with additional black pepper. Serve immediately.

Tuna Fillets with Lemon Butter

Serves: 4 / Prep time: 5 minutes / Cook time: 3 minutes

Ingredients:
- 1 cup water
- ⅓ cup lemon juice
- 2 sprigs fresh thyme
- 2 sprigs fresh parsley
- Sea salt, to taste
- 2 sprigs fresh rosemary
- 1 pound (454 g) tuna fillets
- 4 cloves garlic, pressed
- 1 lemon, sliced
- ¼ teaspoon black pepper, or more to taste
- 2 tablespoons butter, melted

Instructions:
1. Pour water into the Instant Pot and add lemon juice, thyme, parsley, and rosemary. Insert a steamer basket.
2. Place the tuna fillets in the basket, top with garlic, and season with salt and black pepper.
3. Drizzle melted butter over the fish fillets and place lemon slices on top.
4. Secure the lid, select Manual mode, and set the cooking time for 3 minutes at Low Pressure.
5. When the timer beeps, perform a quick pressure release. Carefully remove the lid and serve immediately.

Poached Salmon

Serves: 4 / Prep time: 10 minutes / Cook time: 5 minutes

Ingredients:
- 1 lemon, sliced ¼ inch thick
- 4 (6-ounce / 170-g) skinless salmon fillets, 1½ inches thick
- ½ teaspoon table salt
- ¼ teaspoon pepper

Instructions:
1. Add ½ cup water to Instant Pot. Fold a sheet of aluminum foil into a 16 by 6-inch sling. Arrange lemon slices in two rows across the center of the sling. Sprinkle the flesh side of the salmon with salt and pepper, then place skinned side down on top of the lemon slices.
2. Using the sling, lower the salmon into the Instant Pot, allowing the narrow edges of the sling to rest along the sides of the insert. Lock the lid in place and close the pressure release valve. Select the high-pressure cook function and set the cook time for 3 minutes.
3. Turn off the Instant Pot and quick-release the pressure.

Carefully remove the lid, allowing steam to escape away from you. Using the sling, transfer the salmon to a large plate. Gently lift and tilt the fillets with a spatula to remove the lemon slices. Serve.

Haddock and Veggie Foil Packets

Serves: 4 / Prep time: 5 minutes / Cook time: 10 minutes

Ingredients:

- 1½ cups water
- 1 lemon, sliced
- 2 bell peppers, sliced
- 1 brown onion, sliced into rings
- 4 sprigs parsley
- 2 sprigs thyme
- 2 sprigs rosemary
- 4 haddock fillets
- Sea salt, to taste
- ⅓ teaspoon ground black pepper, or more to taste
- 2 tablespoons extra-virgin olive oil

Instructions:

1. Pour the water and lemon into the Instant Pot and insert a steamer basket.
2. Assemble the foil packets with large sheets of heavy-duty foil.
3. Place the peppers, onion rings, parsley, thyme, and rosemary in the center of each foil. Lay the fish fillets on top of the veggies.
4. Sprinkle with salt and black pepper, then drizzle the olive oil over the fillets. Place the packets in the steamer basket.
5. Lock the lid and set the cooking time for 10 minutes at low pressure on Manual mode.
6. When the timer beeps, perform a quick pressure release. Carefully remove the lid.
7. Serve warm.

Shrimp and Asparagus Risotto

Serves: 4 / Prep time: 15 minutes / Cook time: 20 minutes

Ingredients:

- ¼ cup extra-virgin olive oil, divided
- 8 ounces (227 g) asparagus, trimmed and cut into 1-inch lengths
- ½ onion, chopped fine
- ¼ teaspoon table salt
- 1½ cups Arborio rice
- 3 garlic cloves, minced
- ½ cup dry white wine
- 3 cups chicken or vegetable broth, plus extra as needed
- 1 pound (454 g) large shrimp (26 to 30 per pound), peeled and deveined
- 2 ounces (57 g) Parmesan cheese, grated (1 cup)
- 1 tablespoon lemon juice
- 1 tablespoon minced fresh chives

Instructions:

1. Heat 1 tablespoon of oil in the Instant Pot on the highest sauté function until shimmering. Add asparagus and cook, partially covered, until just crisp-tender, about 4 minutes. Transfer the asparagus to a bowl and set aside.
2. Add the onion, 2 tablespoons oil, and salt to the pot and cook on high sauté until softened, about 5 minutes. Stir in rice and garlic, and cook until the grains are translucent around edges, about 3 minutes. Stir in wine and cook until nearly evaporated, about 1 minute.
3. Add the broth, scraping up any rice stuck to the bottom of the pot. Lock the lid in place, close the pressure release valve, and select high pressure cook for 7 minutes.
4. After the cooking time, quick-release the pressure. Open the lid and stir the shrimp and asparagus into the risotto. Cover and let sit for 5–7 minutes until the shrimp are opaque.
5. Stir in Parmesan and the remaining 1 tablespoon oil. Adjust the consistency with extra hot broth if needed. Stir in lemon juice, season with salt and pepper, and sprinkle with chives before serving.

Perch Fillets with Red Curry

Serves: 4 / Prep time: 5 minutes / Cook time: 6 minutes

Ingredients:

- 1 cup water
- 2 sprigs rosemary
- 1 large lemon, sliced
- 1 pound (454 g) perch fillets
- 1 teaspoon cayenne pepper
- 1 tablespoon butter
- Sea salt and ground black pepper, to taste
- 1 tablespoon red curry paste

Instructions:

1. Add the water, rosemary, and lemon slices to the Instant Pot and insert a trivet.
2. Season the perch fillets with cayenne pepper, salt, and black pepper. Spread the red curry paste and butter over the fillets.
3. Place the fish fillets on the trivet.
4. Lock the lid and set the cooking time for 6 minutes at low pressure on Manual mode.
5. When the timer beeps, perform a quick pressure release. Carefully remove the lid and serve with your favorite keto sides.

Crunchy Fish Bites

Serves: 4 / Prep time: 15 minutes / Cook time: 9 minutes

Ingredients:

- 1 pound (454 g) tilapia fillet
- ½ cup almond flour
- 3 eggs, beaten
- ¼ cup avocado oil
- 1 teaspoon salt

Instructions:

1. Cut the tilapia into small nugget-sized pieces and season with salt.
2. Dip the pieces in beaten eggs, then coat them with almond flour.
3. Heat avocado oil for 3 minutes on Sauté mode.
4. Fry the fish nuggets for 3 minutes on each side or until golden brown.

Chapter 5 Snacks and Appetizers

Asparagus with Herbed Creamy Dip

Serves: 6 / Prep time: 5 minutes / Cook time: 1 minute

Ingredients:
- 1 cup water
- 1½ pounds (680 g) asparagus spears, trimmed

Dipping Sauce:
- ½ cup mayonnaise
- ½ cup sour cream
- 2 tablespoons chopped scallions
- 2 tablespoons fresh chervil
- 1 teaspoon minced garlic
- Salt, to taste

Instructions:
1. Pour the water into the Instant Pot and place a steamer basket inside. Arrange the asparagus spears in the basket.
2. Secure the lid, select the Manual setting, and set the cooking time to 1 minute on High Pressure.
3. Once the timer sounds, release the pressure immediately. Carefully remove the lid and transfer the asparagus to a plate.
4. In a small bowl, whisk together the mayonnaise, sour cream, scallions, chervil, garlic, and salt until smooth.
5. Serve the steamed asparagus with the creamy herb dip on the side.

Green Goddess Bean and Herb Dip

Prep time: 1 minute / Cook time: 45 minutes / Makes 3 cups

Ingredients:
- 1 cup dried navy, great Northern, or cannellini beans
- 4 cups water
- 2 teaspoons fine sea salt
- 3 tablespoons fresh lemon juice
- ¼ cup extra-virgin olive oil, plus 1 tablespoon for drizzling
- ¼ cup fresh parsley leaves, firmly packed
- 1 bunch chives, chopped
- Leaves from 2 tarragon sprigs
- Freshly ground black pepper

Instructions:
1. Add beans, water, and 1 teaspoon of salt to the Instant Pot, stirring until the salt dissolves.
2. Secure the lid and set to high pressure for 30 minutes if using navy or Great Northern beans, or 40 minutes for cannellini beans. The pot will take around 15 minutes to reach full pressure.
3. When cooking finishes, allow pressure to release naturally for 15 minutes, then carefully release

any remaining pressure manually. Drain the beans, reserving ½ cup of the cooking liquid.
4. In a food processor, blend beans, reserved liquid, lemon juice, ¼ cup olive oil, parsley, chives, tarragon, remaining salt, and pepper until smooth.
5. Transfer to a serving dish, drizzle with remaining olive oil, and garnish with pepper. Serve at room temperature or chilled.

Cheesy Pancetta Pizza Dip

Serves: 10 / Prep time: 10 minutes / Cook time: 4 minutes

Ingredients:
- 10 ounces (283 g) Pepper Jack cheese
- 10 ounces (283 g) cream cheese
- 10 ounces (283 g) pancetta, chopped
- 1 pound (454 g) tomatoes, puréed
- 1 cup green olives, pitted and halved
- 1 teaspoon dried oregano
- ½ teaspoon garlic powder
- 1 cup chicken broth
- 4 ounces (113 g) Mozzarella cheese, thinly sliced

Instructions:
1. Combine the Pepper Jack cheese, cream cheese, pancetta, tomatoes, olives, oregano, and garlic powder in the Instant Pot. Pour in the chicken broth.
2. Secure the lid, select the Manual setting, and cook on High Pressure for 4 minutes.
3. When done, quickly release the pressure and carefully open the lid.
4. Spread the Mozzarella slices over the top, close the lid without locking, and allow the cheese to melt in the residual heat.
5. Serve the dip warm and enjoy.

Cheesy Zucchini Bites

Serves: 6 / Prep time: 15 minutes / Cook time: 10 minutes

Ingredients:
- 4 ounces (113 g) Parmesan cheese, grated
- 4 ounces (113 g) Cheddar cheese, grated
- 1 zucchini, grated
- 1 egg, beaten
- 1 teaspoon dried oregano
- 1 tablespoon coconut oil

Instructions:
1. In a bowl, mix the Parmesan, Cheddar, grated zucchini, beaten egg, and oregano until combined.
2. Form small bite-sized rounds with the mixture using your fingertips.
3. Set the Instant Pot to Sauté mode and melt the coconut

oil.

4. Cook the zucchini bites in the oil for about 3 minutes on each side until golden brown.
5. Let them cool slightly and serve warm.

Herbed Zucchini in Tomato Sauce

Serves: 4 / Prep time: 5 minutes / Cook time: 5 minutes

Ingredients:

- 2 tablespoons olive oil
- 2 garlic cloves, chopped
- 1 pound (454 g) zucchini, sliced
- ½ cup water
- ½ cup sugar-free tomato purée
- 1 teaspoon dried thyme
- ½ teaspoon dried rosemary
- ½ teaspoon dried oregano

Instructions:

1. Select Sauté mode on the Instant Pot and heat the olive oil.
2. Add garlic and cook for about 2 minutes until fragrant.
3. Add the zucchini, water, tomato purée, thyme, rosemary, and oregano. Stir to combine.
4. Secure the lid, choose the Manual setting, and set to Low Pressure for 3 minutes.
5. When cooking completes, release pressure quickly and remove the lid with care.
6. Serve the warm zucchini slices immediately.

Pressure-Cooked Garlic Cloves

Serves: 4 / Prep time: 2 minutes / Cook time: 25 minutes

Ingredients:

- 4 bulbs garlic
- 1 tablespoon avocado oil
- 1 teaspoon salt
- Pinch of black pepper
- 1 cup water

Instructions:

1. Trim the tops off each garlic bulb to expose the cloves.
2. Drizzle avocado oil over the tops and season with salt and pepper.
3. Place the garlic bulbs, cut-side up, into a steamer basket or on foil resting on a trivet in the Instant Pot.
4. Secure the lid, seal the vent, and cook on High Pressure for 25 minutes.
5. Quickly release the pressure and allow the garlic to cool slightly.
6. Squeeze out the roasted garlic from the cloves and mash if desired to create a paste.

Italian-Style Sautéed Tomatillos

Serves: 4 / Prep time: 10 minutes / Cook time: 10 minutes

Ingredients:

- 1 tablespoon Italian seasoning

- 4 tomatillos, sliced
- 4 teaspoons olive oil
- 4 tablespoons water

Instructions:

1. Sprinkle Italian seasoning over the tomatillo slices.
2. Heat the olive oil in the Instant Pot on Sauté mode for 1 minute.
3. Place tomatillo slices in the pot in a single layer and cook for 2 minutes on each side.
4. Pour in the water, secure the lid, and cook for 3 more minutes.
5. Serve warm and enjoy the Italian-seasoned tomatillos.

Tuna-Stuffed Deviled Eggs

Serves: 3 / Prep time: 10 minutes / Cook time: 8 minutes

Ingredients:

- 1 cup water
- 6 eggs
- 1 (5 ounces / 142 g) can tuna, drained
- 4 tablespoons mayonnaise
- 1 teaspoon lemon juice
- 1 celery stalk, finely diced
- ¼ teaspoon Dijon mustard
- ¼ teaspoon chopped fresh dill
- ¼ teaspoon salt
- ⅛ teaspoon garlic powder

Instructions:

1. Pour water into the Instant Pot and insert a steamer basket. Place eggs inside and lock the lid. Cook on Manual for 8 minutes.
2. While eggs cook, combine tuna, mayonnaise, lemon juice, celery, mustard, dill, salt, and garlic powder in a bowl.
3. Once done, quick-release the pressure, place eggs in cool water for 10 minutes, then peel.
4. Halve the eggs, remove yolks, and mash them with the tuna mixture until smooth.
5. Spoon the mixture into egg whites and serve chilled.

Spicy Cayenne Beef Cubes

Serves: 6 / Prep time: 5 minutes / Cook time: 23 minutes

Ingredients:

- 2 tablespoons olive oil
- 1 pound (454 g) beef steak, cut into cubes
- 1 cup beef bone broth
- ¼ cup dry white wine
- 1 teaspoon cayenne pepper
- ½ teaspoon dried marjoram
- Sea salt and ground black pepper, to taste

Instructions:

1. Set the Instant Pot to Sauté and warm the olive oil.
2. Add beef cubes and cook for 2-3 minutes, stirring occasionally until lightly browned.
3. Pour in the broth, wine, cayenne, marjoram, salt, and pepper. Stir to mix.

4. Lock the lid and select Manual mode, setting it for 20 minutes on High Pressure.
5. After cooking, allow a natural pressure release for 10 minutes, then release any remaining pressure manually. Carefully open the lid.
6. Transfer the beef to a platter and serve warm.

Mini Taco Beef Bites

Serves: 6 / Prep time: 10 minutes / Cook time: 15 minutes

Ingredients:
- 10 ounces (283 g) ground beef
- 3 eggs, beaten
- ⅓ cup shredded mozzarella cheese
- 1 teaspoon taco seasoning
- 1 teaspoon sesame oil

Instructions:
1. In a bowl, combine ground beef, eggs, mozzarella, and taco seasoning. Mix thoroughly.
2. Shape the mixture into small, bite-sized balls.
3. Heat sesame oil in the Instant Pot on Sauté mode.
4. Place the meatballs in the pot and cook each side for 5 minutes, until golden brown.

Buffalo Chicken Meatballs with Feta

Serves: 4 / Prep time: 5 minutes / Cook time: 10 minutes

Ingredients:
- 1 pound (454 g) ground chicken
- ½ cup almond flour   • 2 tablespoons cream cheese
- 1 packet dry ranch dressing mix
- ½ teaspoon salt   • ¼ teaspoon pepper
- ¼ teaspoon garlic powder
- 1 cup water   • 2 tablespoons melted butter
- ⅓ cup hot sauce   • ¼ cup crumbled feta cheese
- ¼ cup sliced green onion

Instructions:
1. In a large bowl, mix ground chicken, almond flour, cream cheese, ranch mix, salt, pepper, and garlic powder. Shape into 16 meatballs.
2. Place meatballs on a steamer rack in the Instant Pot. Add 1 cup of water and secure the lid. Select the Meat/Stew button and set for 10 minutes.
3. While cooking, mix melted butter with hot sauce in a separate bowl.
4. Once done, quick-release the pressure and transfer meatballs to a clean bowl. Toss with the butter and hot sauce mixture, then top with crumbled feta and green onions.

Asian-Style Ground Turkey Lettuce Wraps

Serves: 8 / Prep time: 5 minutes / Cook time: 30 minutes

Ingredients:
- 3 tablespoons water

- 2 tablespoons soy sauce, tamari, or coconut aminos
- 3 tablespoons fresh lime juice
- 2 teaspoons Sriracha, plus extra for serving
- 2 tablespoons avocado oil
- 2 teaspoons toasted sesame oil
- 4 garlic cloves, minced
- 1-inch piece fresh ginger, minced
- 2 carrots, diced   • 2 celery stalks, diced
- 1 yellow onion, diced • 2 pounds ground turkey
- ½ teaspoon sea salt   • 1 tablespoon cornstarch
- Two 8-ounce cans sliced water chestnuts, drained and chopped
- 2 heads romaine or butter lettuce, leaves separated
- ½ cup roasted cashews, chopped
- 1 cup fresh cilantro leaves

Instructions:
1. In a bowl, combine water, soy sauce, 2 tablespoons lime juice, and Sriracha; set aside.
2. Set the Instant Pot to Sauté and heat avocado oil, sesame oil, garlic, and ginger for 2 minutes. Add carrots, celery, and onion, cooking until the onion softens, about 3 minutes.
3. Add ground turkey and salt, breaking up the meat as it cooks, for about 5 minutes until fully browned. Stir in water chestnuts and soy sauce mixture.
4. Lock the lid and cook on High Pressure for 5 minutes.
5. After cooking, quick-release the pressure and open the pot.
6. In a small bowl, mix remaining lime juice with cornstarch, then add to the pot. Select Sauté and cook until thickened, about 2 minutes.
7. Spoon the turkey mixture onto lettuce leaves, sprinkle with cashews and cilantro, and serve with extra Sriracha.

Garlic-Infused Meatballs

Serves: 6 / Prep time: 20 minutes / Cook time: 15 minutes

Ingredients:
- 7 ounces (198 g) ground beef
- 7 ounces (198 g) ground pork
- 1 teaspoon minced garlic
- 3 tablespoons water
- 1 teaspoon chili flakes
- 1 teaspoon dried parsley
- 1 tablespoon coconut oil
- ¼ cup beef broth

Instructions:
1. In a mixing bowl, combine ground beef, ground pork, minced garlic, water, chili flakes, and dried parsley. Mix thoroughly.
2. Shape the mixture into medium-sized meatballs.
3. Heat coconut oil in the Instant Pot on Sauté mode.
4. Place the meatballs in the pot in a single layer and cook

for 2 minutes on each side until browned.

5. Add beef broth, secure the lid, and select Manual mode. Cook for 10 minutes on High Pressure.

6. Perform a quick pressure release, then transfer the meatballs to a plate for serving.

Warm Colby Cheese and Pepper Dip

Serves: 8 / Prep time: 5 minutes / Cook time: 5 minutes

Ingredients:
- 1 tablespoon butter
- 2 red bell peppers, sliced
- 2 cups shredded Colby cheese
- 1 cup cream cheese, at room temperature
- 1 cup chicken broth
- 2 garlic cloves, minced
- 1 teaspoon red Aleppo pepper flakes
- 1 teaspoon sumac
- Salt and ground black pepper, to taste

Instructions:
1. Set the Instant Pot to Sauté and melt the butter.
2. Add sliced bell peppers and cook for about 2 minutes until they begin to soften.
3. Add Colby cheese, cream cheese, chicken broth, minced garlic, Aleppo pepper flakes, sumac, salt, and pepper, stirring gently to combine.
4. Lock the lid and set to Manual mode, cooking for 3 minutes on High Pressure.
5. Perform a quick pressure release once cooking is complete.
6. Allow to cool for 5 minutes before serving warm.

Bacon-Topped Jalapeño Poppers

Serves: 4 / Prep time: 10 minutes / Cook time: 3 minutes

Ingredients:
- 6 jalapeños
- 4 ounces (113 g) cream cheese
- ¼ cup shredded sharp Cheddar cheese
- 1 cup water
- ¼ cup cooked crumbled bacon

Instructions:
1. Halve the jalapeños lengthwise and remove seeds and membrane. Set aside.
2. In a small bowl, mix cream cheese with Cheddar cheese, then spoon the mixture into each jalapeño half.
3. Add water to the Instant Pot and place a steamer basket inside. Arrange stuffed jalapeños on the rack.
4. Secure the lid, select Manual mode, and cook for 3 minutes on High Pressure.
5. Perform a quick release, then serve jalapeños topped with crumbled bacon.

Cheesy Lemon Cauliflower Bites

Serves: 6 / Prep time: 5 minutes / Cook time: 8 minutes

Ingredients:
- 1 cup water
- 1 pound (454 g) cauliflower, broken into florets
- Sea salt and ground black pepper, to taste
- 2 tablespoons extra-virgin olive oil
- 2 tablespoons lemon juice
- 1 cup grated Cheddar cheese

Instructions:
1. Pour water into the Instant Pot and place a steamer basket inside. Arrange cauliflower florets in the basket.
2. Lock the lid, select Manual mode, and set to cook for 3 minutes on Low Pressure.
3. After cooking, perform a quick release and carefully open the lid.
4. Season cauliflower with salt and pepper, then drizzle with olive oil and lemon juice. Sprinkle grated cheese over the top.
5. Press Sauté mode and cook for about 5 minutes, or until the cheese melts. Serve warm.

Cauliflower Asiago Cheese Balls

Serves: 8 / Prep time: 5 minutes / Cook time: 21 minutes

Ingredients:
- 1 cup water
- 1 head cauliflower, broken into florets
- 1 cup shredded Asiago cheese
- ½ cup grated Parmesan cheese
- 2 eggs, beaten   • 2 tablespoons butter
- 2 tablespoons minced fresh chives
- 1 garlic clove, minced
- ½ teaspoon cayenne pepper
- Coarse sea salt and white pepper, to taste

Instructions:
1. Pour water into the Instant Pot and insert a steamer basket. Add cauliflower florets to the basket.
2. Secure the lid, select Manual mode, and set to cook for 3 minutes on High Pressure.
3. Perform a quick pressure release and carefully open the lid.
4. Transfer cauliflower to a food processor. Add Asiago cheese, Parmesan cheese, eggs, butter, chives, garlic, and cayenne pepper. Pulse until thoroughly combined.
5. Shape the mixture into bite-sized balls and arrange on a baking sheet.
6. Bake in a preheated oven at 400°F (205°C) for 18 minutes, turning the balls halfway through, until golden brown. Cool for 5 minutes before serving.

Sautéed Brussels Sprouts with Aioli Dipping Sauce

Serves: 4 / Prep time: 5 minutes / Cook time: 7 minutes

Ingredients:
- 1 tablespoon butter

- ½ cup chopped scallions
- ¾ pound (340 g) Brussels sprouts

Aioli Sauce:
- ¼ cup mayonnaise
- 1 tablespoon fresh lemon juice
- 1 garlic clove, minced
- ½ teaspoon Dijon mustard

Instructions:
1. Set the Instant Pot to Sauté mode and melt the butter.
2. Add scallions and cook for about 2 minutes until softened. Add Brussels sprouts and sauté for an additional minute.
3. Lock the lid, select Manual mode, and cook for 4 minutes on High Pressure.
4. While sprouts are cooking, mix all Aioli sauce Ingredients in a bowl until well blended.
5. Perform a quick pressure release when cooking ends, and carefully open the lid.
6. Serve the Brussels sprouts with Aioli sauce on the side for dipping.

Crispy Coconut-Crusted Cajun Shrimp

Serves: 2 / Prep time: 10 minutes / Cook time: 6 minutes

Ingredients:
- 4 large tiger shrimp
- 3 tablespoons shredded coconut
- 2 eggs, beaten
- ½ teaspoon Cajun seasoning
- 1 teaspoon olive oil

Instructions:
1. Heat olive oil in the Instant Pot on Sauté mode.
2. In a bowl, combine shredded coconut with Cajun seasoning.
3. Dip each shrimp in beaten eggs, then coat with the coconut mixture.
4. Place the coated shrimp in the heated oil and cook for 3 minutes on each side until golden and crispy.

Broccoli with Garlic and Herb Cheese Sauce

Serves: 4 / Prep time: 5 minutes / Cook time: 3 minutes

Ingredients:
- ½ cup water
- 1 pound (454 g) broccoli, fresh or frozen
- ½ cup heavy cream
- 1 tablespoon butter
- ½ cup shredded Cheddar cheese
- 3 tablespoons garlic and herb cheese spread
- Pinch of salt
- Pinch of black pepper

Instructions:
1. Pour water into the Instant Pot and place the trivet inside. Set a steamer basket on top of the trivet and add broccoli.
2. Lock the lid, seal the vent, and cook on Low Pressure for 1 minute. Quickly release the steam and press Cancel.
3. Remove the steamer basket and drain any remaining water from the pot.
4. Set the pot to Sauté mode, adding cream and butter. Stir until butter melts and cream is warmed.
5. When the cream begins to bubble, add Cheddar cheese, garlic-herb spread, salt, and pepper, stirring until cheeses melt and form a smooth sauce.
6. Spoon the cheese sauce over the broccoli and serve warm.

Creamy Broccoli Cheese Dip

Serves: 6 / Prep time: 5 minutes / Cook time: 10 minutes

Ingredients:
- 4 tablespoons butter
- ½ medium onion, diced
- 1½ cups chopped broccoli
- 8 ounces (227 g) cream cheese
- ½ cup mayonnaise
- ½ cup chicken broth
- 1 cup shredded Cheddar cheese

Instructions:
1. Set the Instant Pot to Sauté mode, then press Adjust to lower the heat to Less. Melt the butter in the pot, add the diced onion, and sauté until softened, about 5 minutes. Press Cancel.
2. Add broccoli, cream cheese, mayonnaise, and chicken broth to the pot. Close the lid and select Manual mode, setting the cook time to 4 minutes.
3. When cooking finishes, quick-release the pressure and open the lid. Stir in the shredded Cheddar until melted and combined.
4. Serve the dip warm and enjoy.

Chicken with Mayo and Celery

Serves: 4 / Prep time: 15 minutes / Cook time: 15 minutes

Ingredients:
- 14 ounces (397 g) skinless, boneless chicken breast
- 1 cup water
- 4 celery stalks
- 1 teaspoon salt
- ½ teaspoon onion powder
- 1 teaspoon mayonnaise

Instructions:
1. Add chicken, water, celery, salt, and onion powder to the Instant Pot.
2. Close the lid, select Manual mode, and cook on High Pressure for 15 minutes.
3. Allow for a natural release for 6 minutes, then release any remaining pressure. Carefully open the lid.

4. Remove the chicken and shred with two forks, then return it to the pot.
5. Stir in the mayonnaise until evenly combined. Serve immediately.

Garlic and Herb Butter

Serves: 4 / Prep time: 10 minutes / Cook time: 8 minutes

Ingredients:
- ⅓ cup butter
- 1 teaspoon dried parsley
- 1 tablespoon dried dill
- ½ teaspoon minced garlic
- ¼ teaspoon dried thyme

Instructions:
1. Preheat the Instant Pot on Sauté mode.
2. Add the butter and allow it to melt.
3. Stir in parsley, dill, minced garlic, and thyme until well combined.
4. Transfer the mixture into a mold and refrigerate until it solidifies.

Cheddar Cheese Crisps

Serves: 4 / Prep time: 10 minutes / Cook time: 5 minutes

Ingredients:
- 1 cup shredded Cheddar cheese
- 1 tablespoon almond flour

Instructions:
1. Combine shredded Cheddar cheese with almond flour in a bowl.
2. Preheat the Instant Pot on Sauté mode.
3. Line the bottom of the Instant Pot with baking paper.
4. Spoon small rounds of the cheese mixture onto the baking paper, then close the lid.
5. Cook on Sauté mode for about 5 minutes or until the cheese has melted and the edges are golden.
6. Turn off the Instant Pot, remove the baking paper with the cheese rounds, and let cool completely before serving.

Creole Cheese and Pancetta Egg Bites

Serves: 6 / Prep time: 5 minutes / Cook time: 5 minutes

Ingredients:
- 1 cup water
- 6 eggs
- 4 slices pancetta, chopped
- ⅓ cup grated Cheddar cheese
- ¼ cup cream cheese
- ¼ cup mayonnaise
- 1 teaspoon Creole seasoning
- Sea salt and ground black pepper, to taste

Instructions:
1. Pour water into the Instant Pot and insert a steamer basket. Place eggs in the basket.

2. Close the lid, select Manual mode, and set to Low Pressure for 5 minutes.
3. When cooking ends, perform a quick pressure release. Carefully open the lid.
4. Allow the eggs to cool for 10 to 15 minutes, then peel and chop them. Transfer to a bowl and mix with pancetta, Cheddar cheese, cream cheese, mayonnaise, and Creole seasoning. Season with salt and pepper.
5. Form the mixture into bite-sized balls and serve chilled.

Creamy Garlic Mashed Cauliflower

Serves: 4 / Prep time: 3 minutes / Cook time: 1 minute

Ingredients:
- 1 head cauliflower, chopped into florets
- 1 cup water
- 1 clove garlic, finely minced
- 3 tablespoons butter
- 2 tablespoons sour cream
- ½ teaspoon salt
- ¼ teaspoon pepper

Instructions:
1. Place cauliflower on a steamer rack inside the Instant Pot. Add water and close the lid. Press the Steam button, setting the time for 1 minute. Quick-release the pressure once cooking is complete.
2. Transfer the cauliflower to a food processor and add garlic, butter, sour cream, salt, and pepper. Blend until smooth and creamy.
3. Serve warm.

Spicy Baked Feta with Peppers and Tomato

Serves: 6 / Prep time: 10 minutes / Cook time: 6 minutes

Ingredients:
- 12 ounces (340 g) feta cheese
- ½ tomato, sliced
- 1 ounce (28 g) bell pepper, sliced
- 1 teaspoon ground paprika
- 1 tablespoon olive oil
- 1 cup water, for cooking

Instructions:
1. Drizzle the feta cheese with olive oil and sprinkle with paprika, then place it on a sheet of foil.
2. Top the feta with sliced tomato and bell pepper, then wrap tightly in the foil.
3. Pour water into the Instant Pot and place the steamer rack inside.
4. Place the wrapped feta on the rack, close the lid, and seal.
5. Select Manual mode and cook on High Pressure for 6 minutes. Quick-release the pressure when done.
6. Carefully unwrap the foil, transfer the feta to serving plates, and enjoy.

Chapter 6 Vegetables and Sides

Curried Cauliflower and Tomato Stew

Serves 4 to 6 / Prep time: 10 minutes / Cook time: 2 minutes

Ingredients:

- 1 medium head cauliflower, cut into bite-size pieces
- 1 (14-ounce / 397-g) can sugar-free diced tomatoes, undrained
- 1 bell pepper, thinly sliced
- 1 (14-ounce / 397-g) can full-fat coconut milk
- ½ to 1 cup water   • 2 tablespoons red curry paste
- 1 teaspoon salt   • 1 teaspoon garlic powder
- ½ teaspoon onion powder
- ½ teaspoon ground ginger
- ¼ teaspoon chili powder
- Freshly ground black pepper, to taste

Instructions:

1. Add all Ingredients, except black pepper, to the Instant Pot and stir well to combine.
2. Close the lid, select Manual mode, and cook on High Pressure for 2 minutes. Once finished, perform a quick pressure release.
3. Open the lid carefully, season with black pepper, and give it a final stir. Serve immediately.

Wild Rice Salad with Dried Cranberries and Toasted Almonds

Serves: 18 / Prep time: 10 minutes / Cook time: 25 minutes

Ingredients:

For the Rice:
- 2 cups wild rice blend, rinsed
- 1 teaspoon kosher salt
- 2½ cups vegetable broth or chicken bone broth

For the Dressing:
- ¼ cup extra-virgin olive oil
- ¼ cup white wine vinegar
- 1½ teaspoons grated orange zest
- Juice of 1 medium orange (about ¼ cup)
- 1 teaspoon honey or pure maple syrup

For the Salad:
- ¾ cup unsweetened dried cranberries
- ½ cup sliced almonds, toasted
- Freshly ground black pepper

Instructions:

1. For the rice, add the wild rice blend, salt, and broth to the Instant Pot. Close and secure the lid, setting the valve to sealing.
2. Select High Pressure and cook for 25 minutes. Once done, cancel and let the pressure naturally release for

15 minutes, then quick-release any remaining pressure.
3. Unlock and open the lid, then fluff the rice with a fork and let it cool briefly.
4. For the dressing, combine olive oil, vinegar, orange zest, juice, and honey in a jar with a lid. Shake well to blend, or whisk together in a bowl if a jar isn't available.
5. In a large bowl, mix the cooked rice, cranberries, and almonds. Pour in the dressing, season with black pepper, and serve warm or chilled.

Hearty Vegetable Curry

Serves: 10 / Prep time: 25 minutes / Cook time: 3 minutes

Ingredients:

- 16-ounce package baby carrots
- 3 medium potatoes, cubed with skins on
- 1 pound fresh or frozen green beans, cut into 2-inch pieces
- 1 medium green bell pepper, chopped
- 1 medium onion, chopped
- 1–2 cloves garlic, minced
- 15-ounce can garbanzo beans, drained
- 28-ounce can crushed tomatoes
- 3 teaspoons curry powder
- 1½ teaspoons chicken bouillon granules
- 1¾ cups boiling water
- 3 tablespoons minute tapioca

Instructions:

1. In the Instant Pot, combine the carrots, potatoes, green beans, bell pepper, onion, garlic, garbanzo beans, crushed tomatoes, and curry powder.
2. Dissolve bouillon in boiling water, then stir in tapioca. Pour this mixture over the vegetables in the Instant Pot, stirring well.
3. Secure the lid, set the vent to sealing, and select Manual mode, cooking on High Pressure for 3 minutes.
4. Once done, manually release the pressure, carefully remove the lid, and serve warm.

Creamy Parmesan Cauliflower Mash

Serves: 4 / Prep time: 7 minutes / Cook time: 5 minutes

Ingredients:

- 1 head cauliflower, cored and cut into large florets
- ½ teaspoon kosher salt
- ½ teaspoon garlic pepper
- 2 tablespoons plain Greek yogurt
- ¾ cup freshly grated Parmesan cheese
- 1 tablespoon unsalted butter or ghee (optional)
- Chopped fresh chives

Instructions:

1. Pour 1 cup of water into the Instant Pot and insert a steamer basket or wire rack.
2. Place the cauliflower florets in the basket.
3. Secure and lock the lid, setting the valve to sealing.
4. Cook on High Pressure for 5 minutes.
5. Once cooking is complete, press Cancel and quick-release the pressure.
6. After the pressure pin drops, unlock and open the lid. Remove the cauliflower from the pot and discard the water.
7. Return the cauliflower to the pot and add salt, garlic pepper, Greek yogurt, and Parmesan. Use an immersion blender or potato masher to puree or mash the cauliflower until smooth.
8. Transfer to a serving bowl, garnish with butter (if desired) and chives, and serve.

Spiced Indian-Style Okra

Serves: 6 / Prep time: 8 minutes / Cook time: 7 minutes

Ingredients:

- 1 pound (454 g) young okra, rinsed, dried, and sliced diagonally into ½ to ¾ inch pieces
- 4 tablespoons ghee or avocado oil
- ½ teaspoon cumin seeds
- ¼ teaspoon ground turmeric
- Pinch of ground cinnamon
- ½ medium onion, diced • 2 cloves garlic, minced
- 2 teaspoons minced fresh ginger
- 1 serrano chile, seeded and minced
- 1 small tomato, diced • ½ teaspoon sea salt
- ¼ teaspoon cayenne pepper (optional)
- 1 cup vegetable stock or filtered water

Instructions:

1. Set the Instant Pot to Sauté mode. Once hot, add ghee and heat until melted. Stir in cumin seeds, turmeric, and cinnamon, cooking until fragrant, about 1 minute.
2. Add the onion and cook, stirring frequently, until softened, about 3 minutes. Add garlic, ginger, and serrano chile, and sauté for an additional minute, then press Cancel.
3. Stir in the diced tomato, okra, salt, cayenne (if desired), and stock. Lock the lid and set the steam release valve to sealing.
4. Select Manual mode and cook on High Pressure for 2 minutes.
5. When the timer beeps, carefully switch the steam release valve to venting to quick-release the pressure.
6. Open the lid and give it a gentle stir. Let the okra rest on Keep Warm for a few minutes before serving.

Green Beans and Potatoes with Fresh Basil

Serves: 4 / Prep time: 20 minutes / Cook time: 10 minutes

Ingredients:

- 2 tablespoons extra-virgin olive oil, plus more for drizzling
- 1 onion, finely chopped
- 2 tablespoons minced fresh oregano or 2 teaspoons dried oregano
- 2 tablespoons tomato paste
- 4 garlic cloves, minced   • ¼ teaspoon pepper
- 1 (14½-ounce / 411-g) can whole peeled tomatoes, drained and chopped (reserve juice)
- 1 cup water   • 1 teaspoon table salt
- 1½ pounds (680 g) green beans, trimmed and cut into 2-inch lengths
- 1 pound (454 g) Yukon Gold potatoes, peeled and cut into 1-inch pieces
- 3 tablespoons chopped fresh basil or parsley
- 2 tablespoons toasted pine nuts
- Shaved Parmesan cheese

Instructions:

1. Using the highest Sauté setting, heat olive oil in the Instant Pot until shimmering. Add onion and cook until softened, about 5 minutes.
2. Stir in oregano, tomato paste, and garlic, cooking until fragrant, about 30 seconds.
3. Add tomatoes with reserved juice, water, salt, and pepper, then stir in green beans and potatoes.
4. Secure the lid, close the pressure release valve, and select High Pressure. Cook for 5 minutes.
5. Once cooking is complete, quick-release the pressure and carefully open the lid.
6. Adjust salt and pepper to taste. Serve garnished with fresh basil, pine nuts, Parmesan, and a drizzle of olive oil.

Moroccan-Style Zucchini

Serves: 4 / Prep time: 10 minutes / Cook time: 6 minutes

Ingredients:

- 2 tablespoons avocado oil
- ½ medium onion, diced
- 1 clove garlic, minced
- ¼ teaspoon cayenne pepper
- ¼ teaspoon ground coriander
- ¼ teaspoon ground cumin
- ¼ teaspoon ground ginger
- Pinch of ground cinnamon
- 1 Roma (plum) tomato, diced
- 2 medium zucchini, cut into 1-inch pieces
- ½ tablespoon fresh lemon juice
- ¼ cup bone broth or vegetable stock

Instructions:

1. Set the Instant Pot to Sauté mode. Once hot, add the avocado oil. Add the onion and sauté, stirring frequently, until translucent, about 2 minutes.

2. Add the garlic, cayenne, coriander, cumin, ginger, and cinnamon. Cook for about 1 minute, until fragrant. Stir in the tomato and zucchini and cook for 2 more minutes.
3. Press Cancel. Add the lemon juice and broth, then secure the lid and set the valve to Sealing. Set the Instant Pot to Manual mode, adjust the pressure to Low, and set the timer for 1 minute.
4. After the cooking time is complete, quick-release the pressure by switching the valve to Venting. Once fully released, carefully open the lid, stir, and serve warm.

Air-Fried Corn on the Cob

Serves: 4 / Prep time: 5 minutes / Cook time: 12 to 15 minutes

Ingredients:
- 2 large ears of fresh corn
- Olive oil for misting
- Salt, to taste (optional)

Instructions:
1. Shuck the corn, remove the silks, and wash thoroughly.
2. Cut each ear in half crosswise.
3. Mist the corn with olive oil.
4. Air fry at 390°F (199°C) for 12 to 15 minutes, or until browned to your liking.
5. Serve plain or with a sprinkle of coarsely ground salt.

Braised Radishes with Snap Peas and Dukkah

Serves: 4 / Prep time: 20 minutes / Cook time: 5 minutes

Ingredients:
- ¼ cup extra-virgin olive oil, divided
- 1 shallot, thinly sliced
- 3 garlic cloves, thinly sliced
- 1½ pounds (680 g) radishes, with 2 cups greens reserved, radishes halved if small or quartered if large
- ½ cup water
- ½ teaspoon table salt
- 8 ounces (227 g) sugar snap peas, strings removed, thinly sliced on the bias
- 8 ounces (227 g) cremini mushrooms, trimmed and thinly sliced
- 2 teaspoons grated lemon zest plus 1 teaspoon lemon juice
- 1 cup plain Greek yogurt
- 3 tablespoons dukkah
- ½ cup fresh cilantro leaves

Instructions:
1. Set the Instant Pot to Sauté on the highest setting and heat 2 tablespoons of olive oil. Add the shallot and cook until softened, about 2 minutes. Stir in garlic and cook until fragrant, about 30 seconds. Add radishes, water, and salt, then lock the lid and set to High Pressure for 1 minute.
2. Turn off the Instant Pot and quick-release the pressure. Open the lid carefully. Stir in snap peas, cover, and let sit for about 3 minutes to warm through.
3. Add radish greens, mushrooms, lemon zest and juice,

and remaining 2 tablespoons of oil. Gently toss to mix. Season with salt and pepper.
4. Spread ¼ cup of yogurt on each of 4 serving plates, spoon the vegetable mixture on top, and sprinkle with cilantro and dukkah. Serve.

Falafel and Lettuce Salad

Serves: 4 / Prep time: 10 minutes / Cook time: 6 to 8 minutes

Ingredients:
- 1 cup shredded cauliflower
- ⅓ cup coconut flour
- 1 teaspoon grated lemon zest
- 1 egg, beaten
- 2 tablespoons coconut oil
- 2 cups chopped lettuce
- 1 cucumber, chopped
- 1 tablespoon olive oil
- 1 teaspoon lemon juice
- ½ teaspoon cayenne pepper

Instructions:
1. Combine the cauliflower, coconut flour, lemon zest, and egg in a bowl. Form the mixture into small balls.
2. Set the Instant Pot to Sauté mode and heat the coconut oil. Place the balls in a single layer in the pot and cook for 3 to 4 minutes per side, until golden brown.
3. In a separate bowl, mix the lettuce, cucumber, olive oil, lemon juice, and cayenne pepper.
4. Serve the cooked falafel on top of the salad and enjoy!

Sauerkraut and Mushroom Casserole

Serves: 6 / Prep time: 6 minutes / Cook time: 15 minutes

Ingredients:
- 1 tablespoon olive oil
- 1 celery rib, diced
- ½ cup chopped leeks
- 2 pounds (907 g) canned sauerkraut, drained
- 6 ounces (170 g) brown mushrooms, sliced
- 1 teaspoon caraway seeds
- 1 teaspoon brown mustard
- 1 bay leaf
- 1 cup dry white wine

Instructions:
1. Set the Instant Pot to Sauté mode. Add olive oil and cook the celery and leeks until softened.
2. Stir in the sauerkraut and mushrooms, cooking for another 2 minutes.
3. Add the caraway seeds, mustard, bay leaf, and white wine. Stir well to combine.
4. Secure the lid, set the Instant Pot to Manual mode on High Pressure, and cook for 10 minutes. Once the cooking time is done, let the pressure release naturally, then carefully remove the lid. Serve warm.

Stir-Fried Asparagus and Kale

Serves: 4 / Prep time: 5 minutes / Cook time: 3 minutes

Ingredients:
- 8 ounces (227 g) asparagus, chopped

- 2 cups chopped kale
- ½ cup water
- 1 teaspoon apple cider vinegar
- ½ teaspoon minced ginger
- 2 bell peppers, chopped
- 1 tablespoon avocado oil

Instructions:
1. Pour water into the Instant Pot.
2. In the Instant Pot pan, combine the asparagus, kale, bell peppers, avocado oil, apple cider vinegar, and ginger.
3. Place the trivet in the Instant Pot and set the pan on top.
4. Close the lid and set the Instant Pot to Manual mode for 3 minutes on High Pressure.
5. Once the timer goes off, perform a quick pressure release. Carefully open the lid and serve immediately.

Curried Cauliflower Rice

Serves: 4 / Prep time: 5 minutes / Cook time: 2 minutes

Ingredients:
- 1 (9-ounce / 255-g) head cauliflower, chopped
- ½ teaspoon garlic powder
- ½ teaspoon freshly ground black pepper
- ½ teaspoon ground turmeric
- ½ teaspoon curry powder
- ½ teaspoon kosher salt
- ½ teaspoon paprika
- ¼ small onion, thinly sliced

Instructions:
1. Add 1 cup of water to the Instant Pot and insert the trivet. Place a greased, Instant Pot-friendly dish inside and fill it with the cauliflower. Sprinkle with garlic powder, black pepper, turmeric, curry powder, salt, paprika, and onion.
2. Place the dish onto the trivet and cover loosely with aluminum foil. Close the lid, set the pressure release valve to sealing, and select Manual mode. Set the Instant Pot to 2 minutes on High Pressure.
3. After the cooking cycle is complete, perform a quick release. Open the lid and remove the dish.
4. Serve immediately.

Lemon Cabbage and Tempeh

Serves: 3 / Prep time: 8 minutes / Cook time: 10 minutes

Ingredients:
- 2 tablespoons sesame oil
- ½ cup chopped scallions
- 2 cups shredded cabbage
- 6 ounces (170 g) tempeh, cubed
- 1 tablespoon coconut aminos
- 1 cup vegetable stock
- 2 garlic cloves, minced
- 1 tablespoon lemon juice
- Salt and pepper, to taste
- ¼ teaspoon paprika
- ¼ cup chopped fresh cilantro

Instructions:
1. Set the Instant Pot to Sauté mode. Heat the sesame oil and sauté the scallions until tender and fragrant.
2. Add the cabbage, tempeh, coconut aminos, vegetable stock, garlic, lemon juice, salt, pepper, and paprika to the pot.
3. Secure the lid, select Manual mode, and set to Low Pressure. Cook for 3 minutes.
4. Once done, use a quick pressure release. After opening the lid, press the Sauté button again to thicken the sauce if desired.
5. Divide into bowls, garnish with cilantro, and serve warm.

Steamed Tomatoes with Halloumi Cheese

Serves: 4 / Prep time: 5 minutes / Cook time: 3 minutes

Ingredients:
- 8 tomatoes, sliced
- 1 cup water
- ½ cup crumbled Halloumi cheese
- 2 tablespoons extra-virgin olive oil
- 2 tablespoons fresh basil, snipped
- 2 garlic cloves, smashed

Instructions:
1. Pour the water into the Instant Pot and place the trivet inside. Arrange the tomato slices on the trivet.
2. Secure the lid, set to Manual mode, and cook on High Pressure for 3 minutes. Once done, quick-release the pressure and carefully open the lid.
3. Toss the cooked tomatoes with the Halloumi cheese, olive oil, basil, and garlic. Serve immediately.

Garlicky Broccoli with Roasted Almonds

Serves 4 to 6 / Prep time: 10 minutes / Cook time: 4 minutes

Ingredients:
- 6 cups broccoli florets
- 1 cup water
- 1½ tablespoons olive oil
- 2 shallots, thinly sliced
- 8 garlic cloves, thinly sliced
- ½ teaspoon crushed red pepper flakes
- Grated zest and juice of 1 medium lemon
- ½ teaspoon kosher salt
- Freshly ground black pepper, to taste
- ¼ cup chopped roasted almonds
- ¼ cup finely slivered fresh basil

Instructions:
1. Pour the water into the Instant Pot and place the broccoli florets in a steamer basket. Lower the basket into the pot.
2. Secure the lid and select the Steam setting. Set the timer for 2 minutes on Low Pressure. After cooking, quick-release the pressure and carefully open the lid.
3. Transfer the broccoli to a bowl of ice water to cool, then drain and pat dry.
4. Set the Instant Pot to Sauté mode. Heat the olive oil, then add garlic and sauté for 30 seconds. Add shallots and pepper flakes, sauté for another minute.
5. Stir in the broccoli, lemon juice, salt, and black pepper. Toss to combine and cook for another minute.

6. Serve the broccoli on a platter, topped with almonds, lemon zest, and basil.

Lemony Brussels Sprouts with Poppy Seeds

Serves: 4 / Prep time: 10 minutes / Cook time: 2 minutes

Ingredients:
- 1 pound (454 g) Brussels sprouts
- 2 tablespoons avocado oil, divided
- 1 cup vegetable broth or chicken bone broth
- 1 tablespoon minced garlic
- ½ teaspoon kosher salt
- Freshly ground black pepper, to taste
- ½ medium lemon
- ½ tablespoon poppy seeds

Instructions:
1. Trim the Brussels sprouts, cutting off the stems and removing any loose outer leaves. Slice each in half lengthwise.
2. Set the Instant Pot to Sauté/More mode and heat 1 tablespoon of avocado oil.
3. Add half of the Brussels sprouts, cut-side down, and let them brown for 3 to 5 minutes without stirring. Transfer to a bowl and repeat with the remaining sprouts.
4. Return all the Brussels sprouts to the pot and add the broth, garlic, salt, and black pepper. Stir to combine.
5. Secure the lid and cook on High Pressure for 2 minutes. After cooking, quick-release the pressure.
6. Zest the lemon, then cut it into quarters.
7. Once the pressure has been released, carefully remove the lid and transfer the Brussels sprouts to a serving bowl.
8. Toss with the lemon zest, a squeeze of lemon juice, and poppy seeds. Serve immediately.

Spaghetti Squash Noodles with Tomatoes

Serves: 4 / Prep time: 15 minutes / Cook time: 14 to 16 minutes

Ingredients:
- 1 medium spaghetti squash
- 1 cup water
- 2 tablespoons olive oil
- 1 small yellow onion, diced
- 6 garlic cloves, minced
- 2 teaspoons crushed red pepper flakes
- 2 teaspoons dried oregano
- 1 cup sliced cherry tomatoes
- 1 teaspoon kosher salt
- ½ teaspoon freshly ground black pepper
- 1 (14.5-ounce / 411-g) can sugar-free crushed tomatoes
- ¼ cup capers
- 1 tablespoon caper brine
- ½ cup sliced olives

Instructions:
1. Slice the spaghetti squash in half, scoop out the seeds, and set aside.

2. Pour water into the Instant Pot and place the trivet in the pot with the handles facing up. Place the squash halves cut-side up on the trivet.
3. Lock the lid and set to Manual mode. Cook on High Pressure for 7 minutes, then quick-release the pressure and carefully open the lid.
4. Remove the trivet and drain the water from the squash cavities. Use a fork to scrape the flesh into spaghetti-like strands and set aside.
5. Pour the water out of the pot and set to Sauté mode. Heat the olive oil, then sauté the onion for 3 minutes.
6. Add garlic, red pepper flakes, and oregano, and sauté for 1 minute.
7. Stir in cherry tomatoes, salt, and black pepper, and cook for 2 minutes, until the tomatoes soften.
8. Pour in the crushed tomatoes, capers, caper brine, and olives. Bring to a boil and cook for 2 to 3 minutes to blend the flavors.
9. Add the spaghetti squash strands to the pot and cook for 1 to 2 minutes to heat through.
10. Serve the dish on a platter and enjoy.

Caramelized Fennel with Radicchio, Pear, and Pecorino

Serves: 4 / Prep time: 20 minutes / Cook time: 12 minutes

Ingredients:
- 6 tablespoons extra-virgin olive oil, divided
- 2 fennel bulbs (12 ounces / 340 g each), fronds chopped, stalks discarded, bulbs halved and cut into 1-inch wedges
- ¾ teaspoon table salt, divided
- ½ teaspoon grated lemon zest, plus 4 teaspoons lemon juice
- 5 ounces (142 g) baby arugula
- 1 small head radicchio (6 ounces / 170 g), shredded
- 1 Bosc or Bartlett pear, quartered, cored, and thinly sliced
- ¼ cup whole almonds, toasted and chopped
- Shaved Pecorino Romano cheese

Instructions:
1. Heat 2 tablespoons of oil in the Instant Pot using the highest sauté setting for about 5 minutes or until it begins to smoke. Brown half of the fennel for around 3 minutes on each side, then transfer to a plate. Repeat with the remaining fennel, using 1 tablespoon of oil, without removing from the pot.
2. Return the first batch of fennel to the pot along with ½ cup water and ½ teaspoon salt. Lock the lid and set the Instant Pot to high pressure for 2 minutes. Perform a quick release and carefully remove the lid.
3. Using a slotted spoon, transfer the fennel to a plate, discarding the liquid.
4. In a large bowl, whisk together the remaining oil,

lemon zest, lemon juice, and the remaining ¼ teaspoon salt. Add the arugula, radicchio, and pear and toss until everything is coated.

5. Transfer the arugula mixture to a serving dish, arranging the fennel wedges on top. Finish by sprinkling almonds, fennel fronds, and Pecorino. Serve immediately.

Cheesy Cauliflower Pasta

Serves: 6 / Prep time: 6 minutes / Cook time: 3 minutes

Ingredients:

- 1 large cauliflower, chopped into bite-sized florets
- 1 cup heavy whipping cream   •   ½ cup sour cream
- 1 cup shredded Gruyère or Mozzarella cheese
- 2½ cups shredded sharp Cheddar cheese
- 1 teaspoon ground mustard   •   1 cup water
- 1 teaspoon ground turmeric   •   Sea salt, to taste
- Pinch of cayenne pepper (optional)

Instructions:

1. Add 1 cup of water to the Instant Pot and insert a metal steaming basket. Place the cauliflower florets inside the basket, secure the lid, and set the steam release valve to sealing. Press Manual and cook on High Pressure for 3 minutes. Once done, perform a quick release.

2. Meanwhile, prepare the cheese sauce by gently simmering the cream in a skillet over medium heat. Whisk in the sour cream until smooth, then gradually add the Gruyère and 2 cups of Cheddar, stirring until melted. Stir in the ground mustard and turmeric, then adjust the salt.

3. Once the cauliflower is cooked, remove it from the pot and toss it in the prepared cheese sauce to coat.

4. Serve warm, garnished with the remaining Cheddar and a pinch of cayenne (optional).

Spicy Whole Cauliflower

Serves: 4 / Prep time: 5 minutes / Cook time: 7 minutes

Ingredients:

- 13 ounces (369 g) cauliflower head   •   1 cup water
- 1 tablespoon coconut cream
- 1 tablespoon avocado oil
- 1 teaspoon ground paprika
- 1 teaspoon ground turmeric
- ½ teaspoon ground cumin   •   ½ teaspoon salt

Instructions:

1. Add water to the Instant Pot and insert the trivet.

2. In a bowl, combine coconut cream, avocado oil, paprika, turmeric, cumin, and salt.

3. Brush the cauliflower head with the coconut cream mixture, ensuring it's well-coated.

4. Place the cauliflower head onto the trivet in the Instant Pot.

5. Lock the lid and set the Instant Pot to Manual mode.

Cook for 7 minutes on High Pressure. After the cooking cycle ends, allow a natural release for 10 minutes, then release any remaining pressure.

6. Open the lid carefully and serve immediately.

Rich and Savory Creamed Kale

Serves: 4 / Prep time: 10 minutes / Cook time: 5 minutes

Ingredients:

- 2 tablespoons extra-virgin olive oil
- 2 cloves garlic, crushed
- 1 small onion, chopped
- 12 ounces (340 g) kale, finely chopped
- ½ cup chicken broth
- 1 teaspoon Herbes de Provence
- 4 ounces (113 g) cream cheese
- ½ cup full-fat heavy cream
- 1 teaspoon dried tarragon

Instructions:

1. Set the Instant Pot to Sauté mode and heat the olive oil. Add the garlic and onion, sautéing for 2 minutes until the onion softens. Stir in the kale, chicken broth, and Herbes de Provence.

2. Lock the lid in place and set the Instant Pot to Manual mode, cooking at High Pressure for 3 minutes. When the timer goes off, release the pressure quickly. Carefully remove the lid.

3. Stir in the cream cheese, heavy cream, and tarragon, mixing until the dish thickens. Serve immediately.

Caramelized Sweet Onions

Serves: 8 / Prep time: 10 minutes / Cook time: 35 minutes

Ingredients:

- 4 tablespoons margarine
- 6 large Vidalia or sweet onions, sliced into thin half rings
- 1 (10-ounce) can chicken or vegetable broth

Instructions:

1. Set the Instant Pot to Sauté mode and melt the margarine. Add the sliced onions and sauté for 5 minutes, stirring occasionally.

2. Pour in the broth and press Cancel to stop the Sauté mode.

3. Lock the lid in place, set the pressure release valve to sealing, and set the Instant Pot to Manual mode. Cook for 20 minutes.

4. Once the cooking time ends, perform a manual pressure release. Open the lid and set the Instant Pot back to Sauté mode. Stir the onions for 10 more minutes, allowing excess liquid to cook off.

Turmeric-Scented Green Cabbage Stew

Serves: 4 / Prep time: 5 minutes / Cook time: 4 minutes

Ingredients:

- 2 tablespoons olive oil

- ½ cup sliced yellow onion
- 1 teaspoon crushed garlic
- Sea salt and freshly ground black pepper, to taste
- 1 teaspoon turmeric powder
- 1 serrano pepper, chopped
- 1 pound (454 g) green cabbage, shredded
- 1 celery stalk, chopped
- 2 tablespoons rice wine
- 1 cup roasted vegetable broth

Instructions:

1. Place all the Ingredients into the Instant Pot.
2. Lock the lid and set the Instant Pot to Manual mode, cooking on High Pressure for 4 minutes. When cooking is complete, perform a quick pressure release.
3. Open the lid carefully and serve the stew immediately in individual bowls.

Cauliflower in Coconut Curry

Serves: 6 / Prep time: 10 minutes / Cook time: 3 minutes

Ingredients:

- 1 pound (454 g) cauliflower, chopped
- 3 ounces (85 g) scallions, chopped
- 1 cup coconut milk
- ¼ cup crushed tomatoes
- 1 tablespoon coconut oil
- 1 teaspoon garam masala
- 1 teaspoon ground turmeric

Instructions:

1. Add the cauliflower, scallions, coconut milk, crushed tomatoes, coconut oil, garam masala, and turmeric to the Instant Pot and stir to combine.
2. Lock the lid, select the Manual mode, and set the cooking time to 3 minutes on High Pressure. After the timer goes off, let the pressure release naturally for 5 minutes before releasing any remaining pressure. Carefully open the lid.
3. Stir the dish well before serving.

Balsamic-Infused Broccoli with Cottage Cheese

Serves: 4 / Prep time: 5 minutes / Cook time: 5 minutes

Ingredients:

- 1 pound (454 g) broccoli, cut into florets
- 1 cup water
- 2 garlic cloves, minced
- 1 cup crumbled cottage cheese
- 2 tablespoons balsamic vinegar
- 1 teaspoon cumin seeds
- 1 teaspoon mustard seeds
- Salt and pepper, to taste

Instructions:

1. Pour the water into the Instant Pot and place the steamer basket inside. Add the broccoli to the basket.

2. Close the lid, set the Instant Pot to Manual mode, and cook for 5 minutes on High Pressure. After the cooking time ends, perform a quick pressure release.
3. Open the lid and stir in the garlic, cottage cheese, balsamic vinegar, cumin seeds, mustard seeds, salt, and pepper.
4. Serve the dish immediately.

Zesty Asparagus with Fresh Gremolata

Serves: 2 to 4 / Prep time: 15 minutes / Cook time: 2 minutes

Ingredients:

Gremolata:
- 1 cup finely chopped fresh Italian flat-leaf parsley leaves
- 3 garlic cloves, peeled and grated
- Zest of 2 small lemons

Asparagus:
- 1½ pounds (680 g) asparagus, trimmed
- 1 cup water

Lemony Vinaigrette:
- 1½ tablespoons fresh lemon juice
- 1 teaspoon Swerve
- 1 teaspoon Dijon mustard
- 2 tablespoons extra-virgin olive oil
- Kosher salt and freshly ground black pepper, to taste

Garnish:
- 3 tablespoons slivered almonds

Instructions:

1. In a small bowl, combine all Ingredients for the gremolata.
2. Pour water into the Instant Pot and arrange the asparagus in a steamer basket. Lower the basket into the pot.
3. Lock the lid and select the Steam mode, setting the timer for 2 minutes on Low Pressure.
4. Meanwhile, prepare the vinaigrette: In a bowl, mix the lemon juice, Swerve, and mustard, whisking to combine. Slowly drizzle in olive oil while whisking continuously. Season with salt and pepper.
5. When the timer ends, perform a quick pressure release. Carefully remove the lid and take the steamer basket out.
6. Transfer the asparagus to a serving platter. Drizzle with the lemon vinaigrette and sprinkle with gremolata. Top with slivered almonds and serve.

Perfectly Roasted Spaghetti Squash

Serves: 4 / Prep time: 5 minutes / Cook time: 7 minutes

Ingredients:

- 1 spaghetti squash (about 2 pounds)

Instructions:

1. Cut the spaghetti squash in half crosswise and scoop out the seeds with a spoon.
2. Add 1 cup of water to the Instant Pot and insert a wire rack or trivet.

3. Place the squash halves, cut-side up, on the rack.
4. Secure and lock the lid, making sure the valve is set to sealing.
5. Set the Instant Pot to cook on high pressure for 7 minutes.
6. Once the cooking time is complete, press Cancel and perform a quick pressure release.
7. After the pressure has been released, unlock the lid.
8. Use tongs to remove the squash halves from the pot and place them on a plate. Once cool enough to handle, scrape the flesh with a fork to separate the strands and discard the skin.

Sautéed Potatoes with Fresh Parsley

Serves: 4 / Prep time: 10 minutes / Cook time: 5 minutes

Ingredients:
- 3 tablespoons margarine, divided
- 2 pounds medium red potatoes (about 2 ounces each), halved lengthwise
- 1 clove garlic, minced   • ½ teaspoon salt
- ½ cup low-sodium chicken broth
- 2 tablespoons chopped fresh parsley

Instructions:
1. Set the Instant Pot to Sauté mode and melt 1 tablespoon of margarine.
2. Add the potatoes, garlic, and salt, stirring well. Sauté for 4 minutes, stirring frequently.
3. Add the chicken broth and mix well.
4. Seal the lid, set the vent to sealing, and select Manual mode for 5 minutes on high pressure.
5. Once the cooking time is up, manually release the pressure.
6. Drain the potatoes, toss them with the remaining margarine and parsley, and serve immediately.

Garlic Lemon Asparagus

Serves: 4 / Prep time: 6 minutes / Cook time: 5 minutes

Ingredients:
- 1 large bunch asparagus, woody ends trimmed
- 1 cup water   • 2 tablespoons salted butter
- 2 large cloves garlic, minced
- 2 teaspoons fresh lemon juice (from ½ lemon)
- ¾ cup finely shredded Parmesan cheese (optional)
- Salt, to taste

Instructions:
1. Cut the asparagus spears on a diagonal into 3 equal pieces, or trim them to fit your Instant Pot.
2. Pour the water into the Instant Pot and place a metal steamer basket inside. Arrange the asparagus in the basket.
3. Secure the lid and set the steam release valve to Sealing. Press the Manual button and cook for 1 minute for tender asparagus (adjust for softer or crisper as desired).
4. Prepare an ice water bath while the asparagus cooks.
5. When the cooking is complete, release the pressure

quickly by switching the valve to Venting. Once the pressure is fully released, open the lid and transfer the asparagus to the ice bath. Let sit for a minute, then drain and pat dry with a towel.
6. Remove the pot insert and wipe dry. Press Sauté and melt the butter in the pot. Add the garlic and sauté for 1 minute.
7. Add the asparagus back into the pot, stirring well to coat with the garlic butter. Add the lemon juice and sauté for an additional minute.
8. Transfer the asparagus to a serving bowl, stir in Parmesan, and season with salt to taste. Serve warm.

Cheddar and Chanterelle Mushrooms

Serves: 4 / Prep time: 10 minutes / Cook time: 5 minutes

Ingredients:
- 1 tablespoon olive oil   • 2 cloves garlic, minced
- 1 (1-inch) ginger root, grated
- 16 ounces (454 g) Chanterelle mushrooms, brushed clean and sliced
- ½ cup unsweetened tomato purée
- ½ cup water   • 2 tablespoons dry white wine
- 1 teaspoon dried basil • ½ teaspoon dried thyme
- ½ teaspoon dried dill weed
- ⅓ teaspoon freshly ground black pepper
- Kosher salt, to taste
- 1 cup shredded Cheddar cheese

Instructions:
1. Press the Sauté button on the Instant Pot and heat the olive oil. Add the garlic and grated ginger, sautéing for 1 minute until fragrant. Stir in the remaining Ingredients, excluding the cheese.
2. Lock the lid, select the Manual mode, and set the cooking time to 5 minutes on Low Pressure. When the timer goes off, perform a quick pressure release. Carefully open the lid.
3. Serve the mushrooms topped with shredded Cheddar cheese.

Perfectly Cooked Brown Rice

Serves: 6 to 12 / Prep time: 5 minutes / Cook time: 22 minutes

Ingredients:
- 2 cups brown rice   • 2½ cups water

Instructions:
1. Rinse the brown rice thoroughly in a fine-mesh strainer.
2. Add the rice and water to the Instant Pot.
3. Secure the lid and set the vent to sealing.
4. Set the Instant Pot to Manual mode and cook on high pressure for 22 minutes.
5. Once cooking is complete, let the pressure release naturally for 10 minutes, then press Cancel and manually release any remaining pressure.

Daikon and Almond Cake

Serves: 12 / Prep time: 10 minutes / Cook time: 45 minutes

Ingredients:
- 5 eggs, beaten
- ½ cup heavy cream
- 1 cup almond flour
- 1 daikon, diced
- 1 teaspoon ground cinnamon
- 2 tablespoons erythritol
- 1 tablespoon butter, melted
- 1 cup water

Instructions:
1. In a mixing bowl, combine eggs, heavy cream, almond flour, ground cinnamon, and erythritol.
2. Add the diced daikon and mix gently with a spatula until well combined.
3. Pour the mixture into a cake pan.
4. Add water to the Instant Pot and place the trivet inside.
5. Set the cake pan on the trivet and carefully lower it into the pot.
6. Close the lid and set the Instant Pot to Manual mode, cooking on High Pressure for 45 minutes.
7. Once cooking is complete, perform a quick pressure release and carefully open the lid.
8. Serve immediately.

Classic Cheesecake

Serves: 8 / Prep time: 30 minutes / Cook time: 45 minutes

Ingredients:
Crust:
- 1½ cups almond flour
- 4 tablespoons butter, melted
- 1 tablespoon Swerve
- 1 tablespoon granulated erythritol
- ½ teaspoon ground cinnamon
Filling:
- 16 ounces cream cheese, softened
- ½ cup granulated erythritol
- 2 eggs
- 1 teaspoon vanilla extract
- ½ teaspoon lemon extract
- 1½ cups water

Instructions:
1. For the crust, combine almond flour, melted butter, Swerve, erythritol, and cinnamon in a bowl. Use a fork to blend until it resembles wet sand.
2. Spray a springform pan with cooking spray, lining the bottom with parchment paper. Press the crust mixture evenly into the bottom and halfway up the sides.
3. Freeze the crust for 20 minutes while preparing the filling.
4. For the filling, beat the cream cheese and erythritol in a stand mixer until light and fluffy, about 2-3 minutes. Add eggs and both extracts, mixing until combined.
5. Remove the crust from the freezer, pour the filling into the crust, and cover the pan with aluminum foil.
6. Pour water into the Instant Pot and place the trivet at the bottom. Lower the pan carefully onto the trivet.
7. Close the lid, select Manual mode, and set the cooking time to 45 minutes on High Pressure.
8. When the timer finishes, perform a quick pressure release, then carefully open the lid.
9. Remove the trivet and cheesecake from the pot. If the center of the cheesecake is still too jiggly, cook for an additional 5 minutes on High Pressure.
10. Allow the cheesecake to cool at room temperature for 30 minutes, then refrigerate for at least 6 hours before removing the pan's sides and slicing.

Vanilla Cream Pie

Serves: 12 / Prep time: 20 minutes / Cook time: 35 minutes

Ingredients:
- 1 cup heavy cream
- 3 eggs, beaten
- 1 teaspoon vanilla extract
- ¼ cup erythritol
- 1 cup coconut flour
- 1 tablespoon butter, melted
- 1 cup water (for cooking)

Instructions:
1. In a mixing bowl, combine coconut flour, erythritol, vanilla extract, eggs, and heavy cream.
2. Grease a baking pan with melted butter.
3. Pour the coconut mixture into the prepared baking pan.
4. Add water to the Instant Pot and place the steamer rack inside.
5. Set the pie on the rack, then close and seal the lid.
6. Cook on Manual mode (High Pressure) for 35 minutes.
7. Let the pressure release naturally for 10 minutes.

Lush Chocolate Cake

Serves: 8 / Prep time: 10 minutes / Cook time: 35 minutes

Ingredients:
For the Cake:
- 2 cups almond flour
- ⅓ cup unsweetened cocoa powder
- 1½ teaspoons baking powder
- 1 cup granulated erythritol
- Pinch of salt
- 4 eggs
- 1 teaspoon vanilla extract
- ½ cup butter, melted and cooled
- 6 tablespoons strong coffee, cooled

- ½ cup water

For the Frosting:
- 4 ounces (113 g) cream cheese, softened
- ½ cup butter, softened
- ¼ teaspoon vanilla extract
- 2½ tablespoons powdered erythritol
- 2 tablespoons unsweetened cocoa powder

Instructions:
1. To make the cake: In a large bowl, whisk together almond flour, cocoa powder, baking powder, erythritol, and salt until well combined.
2. Add eggs and vanilla and mix with a hand mixer until smooth.
3. Gradually add melted butter while mixing on low speed, then mix in coffee. Scrape the sides of the bowl and mix until fully combined.
4. Grease the cake pan with cooking spray and pour the batter into it. Cover the pan tightly with aluminum foil.
5. Add water to the Instant Pot, place the cake pan on the trivet, and carefully lower the pan into the pot.
6. Close the lid and cook on Manual mode for 35 minutes on High Pressure.
7. After cooking, perform a quick pressure release and open the lid.
8. Let the cake cool on a wire rack, then frost once it has cooled completely.
9. To make the frosting: Whip together cream cheese, butter, and vanilla in a medium bowl until light and fluffy.
10. Gradually add powdered erythritol and cocoa powder and continue mixing until well combined.
11. Frost the cooled cake and serve.

Fudgy Walnut Brownies

Serves: 12 / Prep time: 10 minutes / Cook time: 1 hour

Ingredients:
- ¾ cup walnut halves and pieces
- ½ cup unsalted butter, melted and cooled
- 4 large eggs
- 1½ teaspoons instant coffee crystals
- 1½ teaspoons vanilla extract
- 1 cup Lakanto Monkfruit Sweetener Golden
- ¼ teaspoon fine sea salt
- ¾ cup almond flour
- ¾ cup natural cocoa powder
- ¾ cup stevia-sweetened chocolate chips

Instructions:
1. In a small skillet, toast walnuts over medium heat for about 5 minutes, stirring often. Once golden, transfer them to a bowl to cool.
2. Add 1 cup water to the Instant Pot and line a 7-inch round cake pan with parchment paper. Grease the sides of the pan.

3. In a medium bowl, whisk together melted butter, eggs, coffee crystals, vanilla, sweetener, and salt.
4. Mix in almond flour and cocoa powder until combined, then fold in the walnuts and chocolate chips.
5. Pour the batter into the prepared pan, cover tightly with aluminum foil, and place it on a long-handled silicone steam rack.
6. Lower the pan into the Instant Pot, secure the lid, and set the Pressure Release to Sealing.
7. Select Cake, Pressure Cook, or Manual and cook on High Pressure for 45 minutes.
8. After cooking, allow the pressure to release naturally for 10 minutes, then perform a quick release.
9. Carefully remove the pan from the pot and cool for about 2 hours before removing from the pan.
10. Cut into twelve wedges and serve. Store in the refrigerator for up to 5 days or in the freezer for up to 4 months.

Goat Cheese-Stuffed Pears

Serves: 4 / Prep time: 6 minutes / Cook time: 2 minutes

Ingredients:
- 2 ounces goat cheese, at room temperature
- 2 teaspoons pure maple syrup
- 2 ripe, firm pears, halved lengthwise and cored
- 2 tablespoons chopped pistachios, toasted

Instructions:
1. Pour 1 cup of water into the electric pressure cooker and place a wire rack or trivet inside.
2. In a small bowl, mix together the goat cheese and maple syrup.
3. Spoon the goat cheese mixture into the pear halves. Place the pears on the rack inside the pot, cut-side up.
4. Close and lock the lid of the pressure cooker. Set the valve to sealing.
5. Cook on high pressure for 2 minutes.
6. After cooking, press Cancel and quickly release the pressure.
7. Once the pin drops, unlock the lid and carefully remove the pears using tongs.
8. Transfer the pears to serving plates.
9. Top with toasted pistachios and serve immediately.

Chocolate Macadamia Bark

Serves: 20 / Prep time: 5 minutes / Cook time: 20 minutes

Ingredients:
- 16 ounces raw dark chocolate
- 3 tablespoons raw coconut butter
- 2 tablespoons coconut oil
- 2 cups chopped macadamia nuts
- 1 tablespoon almond butter
- ½ teaspoon salt
- ⅓ cup Swerve (or more to taste)

Instructions:

1. In a large bowl, mix together chocolate, coconut butter, coconut oil, macadamia nuts, almond butter, salt, and Swerve until fully combined.
2. Pour 1 cup of water into the Instant Pot and place the trivet inside. Transfer the mixture to a greased Instant Pot-friendly dish.
3. Place the dish on the trivet and cover loosely with aluminum foil. Close the lid, set the valve to Sealing, and select Manual. Set the Instant Pot to cook for 20 minutes on High Pressure.
4. Once the cooking is complete, allow the pressure to release naturally for about 10 minutes, then switch the valve to Venting.
5. Open the Instant Pot, remove the dish, and cool in the refrigerator until set.
6. Once set, break the bark into pieces, serve, and enjoy! Store any leftovers in the refrigerator or freezer.

Candied Mixed Nuts

Serves: 8 / Prep time: 5 minutes / Cook time: 15 minutes

Ingredients:

- 1 cup pecan halves
- 1 cup chopped walnuts
- ⅓ cup Swerve (or more to taste)
- ⅓ cup grass-fed butter
- 1 teaspoon ground cinnamon

Instructions:

1. Preheat the oven to 350°F (180°C) and line a baking sheet with aluminum foil.
2. Add ½ cup filtered water to the Instant Pot, followed by the pecans, walnuts, Swerve, butter, and cinnamon. Stir the mixture, close the lid, and set the pressure valve to Sealing. Set the Instant Pot to cook on Manual mode, High Pressure, for 5 minutes.
3. Once done, perform a quick release by switching the pressure valve to Venting and strain the nuts.
4. Spread the nuts evenly on the prepared baking sheet and bake for 5-10 minutes, or until crisp (watch carefully to avoid burning).
5. Let the nuts cool before serving. Store leftovers in the refrigerator or freezer.

Blackberry Crisp

Serves: 1 / Prep time: 5 minutes / Cook time: 5 minutes

Ingredients:

- 10 blackberries
- ½ teaspoon vanilla extract
- 2 tablespoons powdered erythritol
- ⅛ teaspoon xanthan gum
- 1 tablespoon butter
- ¼ cup chopped pecans
- 3 teaspoons almond flour

- ½ teaspoon cinnamon
- 2 teaspoons powdered erythritol
- 1 cup water

Instructions:

1. Place blackberries, vanilla extract, erythritol, and xanthan gum in a 4-inch ramekin. Stir gently to coat the blackberries.
2. In a small bowl, mix together the remaining Ingredients. Sprinkle this mixture over the blackberries and cover the ramekin with foil.
3. Set the Instant Pot to Manual and cook for 4 minutes. Once the timer beeps, perform a quick pressure release.
4. Serve the crisp warm, optionally adding whipped cream on top.

Coconut Cupcakes

Serves: 6 / Prep time: 5 minutes / Cook time: 10 minutes

Ingredients:

- 4 eggs, beaten
- 4 tablespoons coconut milk
- 4 tablespoons coconut flour
- ½ teaspoon vanilla extract
- 2 tablespoons erythritol
- 1 teaspoon baking powder
- 1 cup water

Instructions:

1. In a mixing bowl, combine eggs, coconut milk, coconut flour, vanilla extract, erythritol, and baking powder.
2. Pour the batter into cupcake molds.
3. Add water to the Instant Pot and place the trivet inside.
4. Carefully place the cupcake molds on the trivet.
5. Close the lid and set to Manual mode, cooking on High Pressure for 10 minutes. Once done, allow a natural pressure release for 5 minutes, then release any remaining pressure.
6. Open the lid carefully and serve immediately.

Almond Butter Keto Fat Bombs

Serves: 6 / Prep time: 3 minutes / Cook time: 3 minutes

Ingredients:

- ¼ cup coconut oil
- ¼ cup no-sugar-added almond butter
- 2 tablespoons cacao powder
- ¼ cup powdered erythritol

Instructions:

1. Press the Sauté button on the Instant Pot and add coconut oil to melt. Once melted, press Cancel and stir in the remaining Ingredients until fully combined. The mixture should be liquid.
2. Pour the mixture into 6 silicone molds and freeze for 30 minutes until set.
3. Store the fat bombs in the fridge.

Fast Chocolate Mousse

Serves: 1 / Prep time: 10 minutes / Cook time: 4 minutes

Ingredients:
- 1 egg yolk
- 1 teaspoon erythritol
- 1 teaspoon cocoa powder
- 2 tablespoons coconut milk
- 1 tablespoon cream cheese
- 1 cup water (for cooking)

Instructions:
1. Add water to the Instant Pot and insert the steamer rack.
2. In a small bowl, whisk together the egg yolk and erythritol until the mixture turns lemon-yellow.
3. Add the coconut milk, cocoa powder, and cream cheese, whisking until smooth.
4. Pour the mixture into a glass jar and place it on the steamer rack.
5. Close and seal the lid. Cook on Manual (High Pressure) for 4 minutes.
6. Once done, perform a quick pressure release.

Berry Cheesecake without Crust

Serves: 12 / Prep time: 10 minutes / Cook time: 40 minutes

Ingredients:
- 16 ounces cream cheese, softened
- 1 cup powdered erythritol
- ¼ cup sour cream
- 2 teaspoons vanilla extract
- 2 eggs
- 2 cups water
- ¼ cup blackberries and strawberries for topping

Instructions:
1. Beat the cream cheese and erythritol in a large bowl until smooth. Add sour cream, vanilla extract, and eggs, mixing gently until well combined.
2. Pour the batter into a 7-inch springform pan. Tap or shake the pan gently to remove air bubbles and level the batter. Cover with foil.
3. Add water to the Instant Pot and place the steam rack inside. Carefully lower the pan into the pot. Set the Instant Pot to the Cake setting and press Adjust to select the More heat option. Set the time for 40 minutes.
4. Once the timer beeps, allow for a full natural pressure release. Carefully lift the pan from the pot using a sling and let it cool before refrigerating.
5. Once cooled, top with blackberries and strawberries and serve.

Key Lime Cheesecake without Crust

Serves: 8 / Prep time: 15 minutes / Cook time: 35 minutes

Ingredients:
- Nonstick cooking spray
- 16 ounces light cream cheese (Neufchâtel), softened
- ⅔ cup granulated erythritol
- ¼ cup unsweetened Key lime juice
- ½ teaspoon vanilla extract
- ¼ cup plain Greek yogurt
- 1 teaspoon grated lime zest
- 2 large eggs
- Whipped cream, for garnish (optional)

Instructions:
1. Spray a 7-inch springform pan with nonstick cooking spray. Line the bottom and partway up the sides with foil.
2. In a large bowl, beat the cream cheese with an electric mixer until smooth, about 2 minutes. Add erythritol, lime juice, vanilla, yogurt, and zest, blending until smooth. Scrape down the sides of the bowl. Add eggs one at a time, mixing just until incorporated.
3. Pour the mixture into the prepared pan. Drape a paper towel over the top of the pan, then wrap it tightly in foil to keep moisture out.
4. Add 1 cup of water to the Instant Pot. Place the foil-covered pan onto the wire rack and carefully lower it into the pot.
5. Close and lock the lid, setting the valve to sealing. Cook on High Pressure for 35 minutes.
6. Once the cooking time is complete, let the pressure release naturally for 20 minutes, then perform a quick release.
7. Once the pin drops, unlock the lid and carefully transfer the pan to a cooling rack. Let it cool to room temperature, then refrigerate for at least 3 hours.
8. To serve, run a thin spatula around the edge of the cheesecake to loosen it, then remove the ring. Slice and serve with whipped cream, if desired.

Pine Nut Mousse

Serves: 8 / Prep time: 5 minutes / Cook time: 35 minutes

Ingredients:
- 1 tablespoon butter
- 1¼ cups pine nuts
- 1¼ cups full-fat heavy cream
- 2 large eggs
- 1 teaspoon vanilla extract
- 1 cup Swerve (reserve 1 tablespoon)
- 1 cup water
- 1 cup heavy whipping cream

Instructions:
1. Butter the bottom and sides of a pie pan and set aside.
2. Blend the pine nuts and heavy cream in a food processor until smooth. Add eggs, vanilla, and Swerve and pulse to incorporate.
3. Pour the mixture into the prepared pan and cover loosely with foil. Add water to the Instant Pot and place the trivet inside. Lower the pan onto the trivet.
4. Close the lid and select Manual mode, cooking for 35

minutes on High Pressure.

5. In a separate bowl, whisk the heavy whipping cream and 1 tablespoon of Swerve until soft peaks form.

6. Once the timer beeps, let the pressure release naturally for 15 minutes, then release any remaining pressure.

7. Serve the mousse immediately topped with whipped cream.

Espresso Chocolate Cream

Serves: 4 / Prep time: 10 minutes / Cook time: 9 minutes

Ingredients:
- 1 cup heavy cream
- ½ teaspoon espresso powder
- ½ teaspoon vanilla extract
- 2 teaspoons unsweetened cocoa powder
- ¼ cup low-carb chocolate chips
- ½ cup powdered erythritol
- 3 egg yolks
- 1 cup water

Instructions:
1. Set your Instant Pot to Sauté and combine the heavy cream, espresso powder, vanilla extract, and cocoa powder. Bring the mixture to a boil, then stir in the chocolate chips until fully melted. Press Cancel to stop the sauté function.

2. In a separate bowl, whisk together the erythritol and egg yolks. Slowly incorporate this mixture into the melted chocolate blend in the Instant Pot. Pour the combined mixture into four small ramekins.

3. Rinse and replace the inner pot. Pour 1 cup of water into the pot and insert the steam rack. Place the ramekins on the rack and cover them loosely with aluminum foil. Seal the Instant Pot lid.

4. Set to Manual mode for 9 minutes on High Pressure. Let the pressure release naturally. Once the pin drops, carefully open the lid and remove the ramekins. Allow to cool to room temperature, then refrigerate until chilled. Serve with whipped cream if desired.

Coconut Lemon Bars

Serves: 5 to 6 / Prep time: 5 minutes / Cook time: 40 minutes

Ingredients:
- 3 eggs
- 2 tablespoons grass-fed butter, softened
- ½ cup full-fat coconut milk
- ½ teaspoon baking powder
- ½ teaspoon vanilla extract
- ½ cup Swerve (or more to taste)
- ¼ cup lemon juice
- 1 cup blanched almond flour

Instructions:
1. In a bowl, whisk together the eggs, butter, coconut milk, baking powder, vanilla extract, Swerve, lemon juice, and almond flour until smooth.

2. Add 1 cup of filtered water to the Instant Pot and place the trivet inside. Grease an Instant Pot-safe dish, then pour the batter into it.

3. Using a sling, carefully lower the dish onto the trivet inside the pot and cover with aluminum foil. Secure the lid and set to Manual mode for 40 minutes on High Pressure.

4. Allow the pressure to release naturally for 10 minutes before switching to Venting.

5. Carefully remove the dish, let it cool, then cut into 6 squares and serve.

Pumpkin Bundt Cake with Glaze

Serves: 12 / Prep time: 7 minutes / Cook time: 35 minutes

Ingredients:
For the cake:
- 3 cups blanched almond flour
- 1 teaspoon baking soda
- ½ teaspoon sea salt
- 2 teaspoons ground cinnamon
- 1 teaspoon ground nutmeg
- 1 teaspoon ginger powder
- ¼ teaspoon ground cloves
- 6 large eggs
- 2 cups pumpkin puree
- 1 cup Swerve
- ¼ cup unsalted butter (or coconut oil for dairy-free), softened

For the glaze:
- 1 cup unsalted butter (or coconut oil for dairy-free), melted
- ½ cup Swerve

Instructions:
1. In a large bowl, stir together almond flour, baking soda, salt, and spices. In another bowl, mix the eggs, pumpkin puree, sweetener, and butter until smooth. Combine the wet and dry Ingredients and mix well.

2. Grease a 6-cup Bundt pan and pour the batter into it. Cover with a paper towel and aluminum foil.

3. Add 2 cups of cold water to the Instant Pot and place the trivet inside. Lower the Bundt pan onto the trivet.

4. Lock the lid and set the Instant Pot to Manual mode, cooking for 35 minutes on High Pressure.

5. After cooking, allow the pressure to naturally release for 10 minutes, then carefully open the lid.

6. Let the cake cool in the pot for 10 minutes before removing it.

7. While the cake cools, prepare the glaze by mixing melted butter and Swerve. Spoon the glaze over the warm cake.

8. Let the cake cool for another 5 minutes before slicing and serving.

Ricotta and Lemon Cake

Serves: 12 / Prep time: 15 minutes / Cook time: 35 minutes

Ingredients:
- Cooking spray
- 1⅓ cups Swerve
- ½ cup (1 stick) unsalted butter, softened
- 2 teaspoons lemon or vanilla extract
- 5 large eggs, separated
- 2½ cups blanched almond flour
- 1¼ cups (10 oz / 284 g) whole-milk ricotta cheese
- ¼ cup lemon juice
- 1 cup cold water

Instructions:
1. Spray a baking pan with cooking spray and set aside.
2. In a stand mixer, combine the Swerve, butter, and extract. Blend for 8 to 10 minutes until smooth, scraping the bowl as needed.
3. Add the egg yolks and mix until well combined. Then, stir in the almond flour, ricotta cheese, and lemon juice.
4. In a separate bowl, whisk the egg whites until stiff peaks form. Gently fold the egg whites into the batter. Pour into the prepared pan and smooth the top.
5. Add 1 cup of water to the Instant Pot, place the trivet inside, and use a foil sling to lower the pan onto the trivet. Secure the lid.
6. Set the Instant Pot to Manual mode and cook for 30 minutes on High Pressure. Let the pressure release naturally for 10 minutes.
7. Carefully remove the lid, use the sling to lift the pan out, and let it chill in the fridge for 40 minutes.
8. For the glaze, heat the butter in a pan for 5 minutes until it turns brown. Stir in Swerve, lemon juice, and cream cheese. Let cool until it thickens.
9. Pour the glaze over the chilled cake, garnish with lemon zest, and refrigerate for 30 more minutes before serving.

Vanilla Custard Brûlée

Serves: 4 / Prep time: 7 minutes / Cook time: 9 minutes

Ingredients:
- 1 cup heavy cream (or full-fat coconut milk for dairy-free)
- 2 large egg yolks
- 2 tablespoons Swerve (or more to taste)
- Seeds scraped from ½ vanilla bean (or 1 teaspoon vanilla extract)
- 1 cup cold water
- 4 teaspoons Swerve (for topping)

Instructions:
1. Heat the cream in a pan over medium-high heat for about 2 minutes until hot.
2. Blend the egg yolks, Swerve, and vanilla in a blender until smooth. While blending, slowly pour in the hot cream. Taste and adjust sweetness if needed.
3. Spoon the custard mixture into four ramekins. Cover with aluminum foil.
4. Add 1 cup of water to the Instant Pot and insert the trivet. Place the ramekins on the trivet and seal the lid.
5. Set the Instant Pot to Manual mode for 7 minutes on High Pressure.
6. Once done, perform a quick pressure release, carefully remove the lid, and uncover the ramekins. Chill in the fridge for 2 hours.
7. When ready to serve, sprinkle 1 teaspoon of Swerve on each custard and use a broiler to caramelize the top. Let cool for 5 minutes before serving.

Caramelized Pumpkin Cheesecake

Serves: 8 / Prep time: 15 minutes / Cook time: 45 minutes

Ingredients:

Crust:
- 1½ cups almond flour
- 4 tablespoons butter, melted
- 1 tablespoon Swerve
- 1 tablespoon granulated erythritol
- ½ teaspoon ground cinnamon
- Cooking spray

Filling:
- 16 ounces (454 g) cream cheese, softened
- ½ cup granulated erythritol
- 2 eggs
- ¼ cup pumpkin purée
- 3 tablespoons Swerve
- 1 teaspoon vanilla extract
- ¼ teaspoon pumpkin pie spice
- 1½ cups water

Instructions:
1. For the crust, mix almond flour, melted butter, Swerve, erythritol, and cinnamon in a bowl. Use a fork to blend together.
2. Spray the pan with cooking spray and line the bottom with parchment paper.
3. Press the crust evenly into the pan and up the sides halfway, ensuring no bare spots remain.
4. Freeze the crust for 20 minutes while preparing the filling.
5. For the filling, beat together cream cheese and erythritol with a hand mixer until fluffy, about 2-3 minutes.
6. Add eggs, pumpkin purée, Swerve, vanilla, and pumpkin pie spice. Mix until fully incorporated.
7. Remove the crust from the freezer and pour the filling over it. Cover the pan with foil and place it on a trivet.
8. Add water to the Instant Pot and carefully lower the trivet with the pan inside.
9. Close the lid and set the Instant Pot to Manual for 45

minutes on High Pressure. After cooking, perform a quick pressure release.

10. Open the lid carefully. The cheesecake's center should be slightly jiggly.
11. Cool the cheesecake on the counter for 30 minutes before transferring it to the fridge for at least 6 hours.
12. Once set, remove the sides of the pan and serve.

Keto Brownies

Serves: 8 / Prep time: 15 minutes / Cook time: 15 minutes

Ingredients:

- 1 cup coconut flour
- 1 tablespoon cocoa powder
- 1 tablespoon coconut oil
- 1 teaspoon vanilla extract
- 1 teaspoon baking powder
- 1 teaspoon apple cider vinegar
- ⅓ cup butter, melted
- 1 tablespoon erythritol
- 1 cup water

Instructions:

1. In a bowl, combine erythritol, melted butter, apple cider vinegar, baking powder, vanilla, coconut oil, cocoa powder, and coconut flour.
2. Whisk the mixture until smooth and pour into a greased baking pan. Flatten the surface of the batter.
3. Add water to the Instant Pot and place the steamer rack inside.
4. Place the brownie pan on the rack and close the lid, sealing it.
5. Set the Instant Pot to Manual mode (High Pressure) for 15 minutes.
6. After cooking, let the pressure release naturally for 5 minutes.
7. Cut the brownies into bars once they've cooled.

Coconut Delight Bars

Serves: 2 / Prep time: 15 minutes / Cook time: 4 minutes

Ingredients:

- ⅓ cup coconut flakes
- 1 tablespoon butter
- 1 egg, beaten
- 1 cup water (for cooking)

Instructions:

1. Mix together the coconut flakes, butter, and beaten egg.
2. Transfer the mixture into a square mold and press it down evenly.
3. Add water to the Instant Pot and place the steamer rack inside.
4. Place the mold with the mixture on the rack, seal the lid, and cook on Manual mode (High Pressure) for 4 minutes.
5. Release the pressure quickly once done.
6. Let the dessert cool slightly, then cut into squares.

Nutmeg Cupcakes

Serves: 7 / Prep time: 5 minutes / Cook time: 30 minutes

Ingredients:

Cake:
- 2 cups blanched almond flour
- 2 tablespoons grass-fed butter, softened
- 2 eggs
- ½ cup unsweetened almond milk
- ½ cup Swerve, or more to taste
- ½ teaspoon ground nutmeg
- ½ teaspoon baking powder

Frosting:
- 4 ounces (113 g) full-fat cream cheese, softened
- 4 tablespoons grass-fed butter, softened
- 2 cups heavy whipping cream
- 1 teaspoon vanilla extract
- ½ cup Swerve, or more to taste
- 6 tablespoons sugar-free chocolate chips (optional)

Instructions:

1. Pour 1 cup of filtered water into the Instant Pot and insert the trivet. In a large bowl, mix almond flour, butter, eggs, almond milk, Swerve, nutmeg, and baking powder.
2. Transfer the batter into greased, Instant Pot-friendly molds.
3. Place the molds onto the trivet and cover loosely with foil.
4. Set the Instant Pot to Manual for 30 minutes on High Pressure.
5. In the meantime, prepare the frosting by mixing cream cheese, butter, whipping cream, vanilla, and Swerve with an electric hand mixer until light and fluffy. Refrigerate the frosting.
6. After the cupcakes cook, let the pressure release naturally for 10 minutes. Then, release the remaining pressure.
7. Remove the cupcakes and let them cool. Once cooled, top each with a dollop of frosting.

Chocolate Pecan Clusters

Prep time: 5 minutes / Cook time: 5 minutes / Makes 8 clusters

Ingredients:

- 3 tablespoons butter
- ¼ cup heavy cream
- 1 teaspoon vanilla extract
- 1 cup chopped pecans
- ¼ cup low-carb chocolate chips

Instructions:

1. Press the Sauté button on the Instant Pot and melt the butter, allowing it to turn golden brown. Once it starts to brown, add the heavy cream and press Cancel.
2. Stir in the vanilla extract and chopped pecans. Let the mixture cool for about 10 minutes, stirring

occasionally.

3. Spoon the mixture onto a parchment-lined baking sheet to form 8 clusters. Scatter chocolate chips over the top.
4. Place the baking sheet in the fridge to cool and set.

Spicy Chipotle Black Bean Brownies

Serves: 8 / Prep time: 15 minutes / Cook time: 30 minutes

Ingredients:
- Nonstick cooking spray
- ½ cup dark chocolate chips, divided
- ¾ cup cooked black or calypso beans
- ½ cup extra-virgin olive oil
- 2 large eggs
- ¼ cup unsweetened dark cocoa powder
- ⅓ cup honey
- 1 teaspoon vanilla extract
- ⅓ cup white wheat flour
- ½ teaspoon chipotle chili powder
- ½ teaspoon ground cinnamon
- ½ teaspoon baking powder
- ½ teaspoon kosher salt

Instructions:
1. Lightly coat a 7-inch Bundt pan with nonstick spray.
2. In a small bowl, microwave half the chocolate chips in 30-second bursts, stirring until melted.
3. Blend the black beans and olive oil in a food processor. Add the melted chocolate, eggs, cocoa powder, honey, and vanilla. Process until smooth.
4. In a large bowl, mix the flour, chipotle chili powder, cinnamon, baking powder, and salt. Stir in the bean mixture and combine thoroughly.
5. Fold in the remaining chocolate chips.
6. Pour the batter into the Bundt pan and loosely cover with foil.
7. Pour 1 cup of water into the Instant Pot and insert the wire rack.
8. Place the Bundt pan on the rack and lower it into the pot.
9. Seal the lid, set the valve to sealing, and cook on high pressure for 30 minutes.
10. Once done, press Cancel and quickly release the pressure.
11. When the pin drops, carefully remove the lid.
12. After 10 minutes, transfer the pan to a cooling rack. Invert the pan to cool completely.
13. Slice into pieces and serve.

Creamy Vanilla Butter Curd

Serves: 3 / Prep time: 5 minutes / Cook time: 6 hours

Ingredients:
- 4 egg yolks, whisked
- 1 tablespoon erythritol
- ½ cup organic almond milk
- 1 teaspoon vanilla extract
- 2 tablespoons butter

Instructions:
1. Set the Instant Pot to Sauté mode. When it reads "Hot," add the butter.
2. Melt the butter without letting it boil, then stir in the egg yolks, almond milk, and vanilla.
3. Add the erythritol and whisk until well mixed.
4. Cook on Low heat for 6 hours, stirring occasionally.

Raspberry Espresso Cheesecake

Serves: 8 / Prep time: 5 minutes / Cook time: 35 minutes

Ingredients:
- 1 cup blanched almond flour
- ½ cup plus 2 tablespoons Swerve
- 3 tablespoons espresso powder, divided
- 2 tablespoons butter
- 1 egg
- ½ cup full-fat heavy cream
- 16 ounces (454 g) cream cheese
- 1 cup water
- 6 ounces (170 g) dark chocolate (at least 80% cacao)
- 8 ounces (227 g) full-fat heavy whipping cream
- 2 cups raspberries

Instructions:
1. In a small bowl, mix the almond flour, 2 tablespoons of Swerve, 1 tablespoon of espresso powder, and melted butter.
2. Line the bottom of a springform pan with parchment paper. Press the almond flour mixture into the bottom, spreading it about 1 inch up the sides.
3. In a food processor, combine the egg, heavy cream, cream cheese, remaining Swerve, and remaining espresso powder. Blend until smooth.
4. Pour the cheesecake mixture into the prepared pan. Cover loosely with foil.
5. Add water to the Instant Pot and place a trivet inside.
6. Close the lid, set the valve to sealing, and cook on high pressure for 35 minutes.
7. Once the cooking is complete, let the pressure release naturally for 15 minutes, then release any remaining pressure. Open the lid.
8. Remove the pan from the Instant Pot and place it on a cooling rack for 2–3 hours to cool to room temperature.
9. Refrigerate overnight.
10. Melt the dark chocolate with heavy cream in a double boiler. Let it cool for 15 minutes, then drizzle over the cheesecake.
11. Top with fresh raspberries before serving.

Berry Tapioca Parfaits

Serves: 4 / Prep time: 10 minutes / Cook time: 6 minutes

Ingredients:
- 2 cups unsweetened almond milk
- ½ cup small pearl tapioca, rinsed and still wet
- 1 teaspoon almond extract
- 1 tablespoon pure maple syrup

- 2 cups mixed berries   • ¼ cup slivered almonds

Instructions:

1. Pour the almond milk into the Instant Pot and stir in the tapioca and almond extract.
2. Close and seal the lid, setting the valve to sealing.
3. Cook on high pressure for 6 minutes.
4. Once cooking is finished, press Cancel and let the pressure naturally release for 10 minutes, then use quick release for any remaining pressure.
5. After the pin drops, remove the lid and set the pot on a cooling rack.
6. Stir in the maple syrup and let it cool for about an hour.
7. Layer the tapioca, berries, and almonds into small glasses. Refrigerate for 1 hour.
8. Serve chilled.

Strawberry Coconut Cheesecake

Serves: 2 / Prep time: 20 minutes / Cook time: 10 minutes

Ingredients:

- 1 tablespoon gelatin
- 4 tablespoons water (for gelatin)
- 4 tablespoons cream cheese
- 1 strawberry, chopped   • ¼ cup coconut milk
- 1 tablespoon Swerve

Instructions:

1. Mix the gelatin with water and let it sit for 10 minutes.
2. Pour coconut milk into the Instant Pot and bring to a boil on Sauté mode, about 10 minutes.
3. Meanwhile, mash the strawberry and mix it with the cream cheese.
4. Add the strawberry-cream cheese mixture to the hot coconut milk and stir until smooth.
5. Let the mixture cool for 10 minutes, then whisk in the gelatin until it dissolves.
6. Pour the cheesecake mixture into molds and freeze for 3 hours.

Lemon Ricotta Cheesecake

Serves: 6 / Prep time: 10 minutes / Cook time: 30 minutes

Ingredients:

- Unsalted butter or vegetable oil for greasing the pan
- 8 ounces (227 g) cream cheese, softened
- ¼ cup plus 1 teaspoon Swerve (adjust to taste)
- ⅓ cup full-fat or part-skim ricotta cheese, softened
- Zest of 1 lemon   • Juice of 1 lemon
- ½ teaspoon lemon extract
- 2 eggs, room temperature
- 2 tablespoons sour cream

Instructions:

1. Thoroughly grease a 6-inch springform pan with butter or oil, or line the sides with parchment paper.
2. In a stand mixer, blend cream cheese, ¼ cup of Swerve, ricotta, lemon zest, lemon juice, and lemon extract on

high speed until smooth and free of lumps.
3. Taste the mixture and add more Swerve if you desire a sweeter cheesecake.
4. Add the eggs, then lower the mixer speed to low and mix until the eggs are just incorporated. Be careful not to overbeat to avoid cracks.
5. Pour the batter into the prepared pan and cover with foil or a silicone lid.
6. Pour 2 cups of water into the Instant Pot and insert the trivet. Place the pan on the trivet.
7. Lock the lid and set the pressure to High. Cook for 30 minutes, then allow the pressure to naturally release. Unlock the lid.
8. Carefully remove the pan from the Instant Pot, discard the foil, and set it aside.
9. Mix the sour cream with the remaining 1 teaspoon of Swerve and spread over the warm cheesecake.
10. Chill the cheesecake in the refrigerator for 6 to 8 hours before serving.

Pecan Pumpkin Pie

Serves 5 to 6 / Prep time: 5 minutes / Cook time: 40 minutes

Ingredients:

Base:
- 2 tablespoons grass-fed butter, softened
- 1 cup blanched almond flour
- ½ cup chopped pecans

Topping:
- ½ cup Swerve, or to taste
- ⅓ cup heavy whipping cream
- ½ teaspoon ground cinnamon
- ½ teaspoon finely grated ginger
- ½ teaspoon ground nutmeg
- ½ teaspoon ground cloves
- 1 (14-ounce / 397-g) can organic pumpkin purée
- 1 egg

Instructions:

1. Add 1 cup of filtered water to the Instant Pot and place the trivet inside. In a bowl, combine butter, almond flour, and chopped pecans using an electric mixer. Press this mixture into a well-greased, Instant Pot-safe pan to form a crust. Freeze for 15 minutes.
2. While the crust is freezing, mix all the topping Ingredients in a large bowl until well combined.
3. After 15 minutes, take the crust from the freezer and pour the topping mixture over it. Place the pan on the trivet and cover loosely with foil.
4. Close the Instant Pot lid, set the valve to sealing, and select Manual. Cook on High Pressure for 40 minutes. Let the pressure release naturally for 10 minutes, then carefully switch to Venting.
5. Open the lid and remove the pan. Let the pie cool in the fridge for 4 to 5 hours before serving.

Chapter 8 Stews and Soups

Chicken and Mushroom Soup

Serves: 4 / Prep time: 5 minutes / Cook time: 15 minutes

Ingredients:
- 1 onion, sliced thinly
- 3 garlic cloves, minced
- 2 cups chopped mushrooms
- 1 yellow summer squash, chopped
- 1 pound (454 g) boneless, skinless chicken breast, cut into chunks
- 2½ cups chicken broth
- 1 teaspoon salt
- 1 teaspoon freshly ground black pepper
- 1 teaspoon Italian seasoning or poultry seasoning
- 1 cup heavy cream

Instructions:
1. Place the onion, garlic, mushrooms, squash, chicken, chicken broth, salt, pepper, and Italian seasoning in the Instant Pot inner pot.
2. Lock the lid, set the pressure to High, and select Manual. Cook for 15 minutes. Once done, let the pressure release naturally for 10 minutes, then quick-release any remaining pressure. Unlock the lid.
3. Using tongs, transfer the chicken to a bowl and set aside.
4. Tilt the pot slightly, then use an immersion blender to purée the vegetables, leaving some pieces intact for texture.
5. Shred the chicken and return it to the soup.
6. Stir in the cream, mixing well. Serve hot.

Buttercup Squash Soup

Serves: 6 / Prep time: 15 minutes / Cook time: 10 minutes

Ingredients:
- 2 tablespoons extra-virgin olive oil
- 1 medium onion, chopped
- 4 to 5 cups vegetable broth or chicken bone broth
- 1½ pounds buttercup squash, peeled, seeded, and cut into 1-inch chunks
- ½ teaspoon kosher salt
- ¼ teaspoon ground white pepper
- Whole nutmeg, for grating

Instructions:
1. Set the Instant Pot to Sauté. When hot, add olive oil.
2. Add the onion and sauté for 3–5 minutes until softened. Press Cancel to stop sautéing.
3. Add the broth, squash, salt, and pepper, stirring to combine. (For thicker soup, use 4 cups of broth; for thinner soup, use 5 cups.)
4. Close and lock the lid, setting the vent to sealing.
5. Cook on high pressure for 10 minutes.
6. Once cooking is complete, press Cancel and let the pressure release naturally.
7. When the pin drops, unlock the lid and remove it.
8. Use an immersion blender to purée the soup in the pot. Alternatively, transfer it to a blender or food processor and purée.
9. Serve the soup in bowls and grate fresh nutmeg on top.

Creamy Chicken Wild Rice Soup

Serves: 5 / Prep time: 15 minutes / Cook time: 15 minutes

Ingredients:
- 2 tablespoons margarine
- ½ cup diced yellow onion
- ¾ cup diced carrots
- ¾ cup sliced mushrooms (about 3–4 mushrooms)
- ½ pound diced chicken breast (1-inch cubes)
- 6.2-ounce box Uncle Ben's Long Grain & Wild Rice Fast Cook
- 2 (14-ounce) cans low-sodium chicken broth
- 1 cup skim milk
- 1 cup evaporated skim milk
- 2 ounces fat-free cream cheese
- 2 tablespoons cornstarch

Instructions:
1. Set the Instant Pot to Sauté. Add margarine, onion, carrots, and mushrooms. Sauté for about 5 minutes until the onions are soft.
2. Add cubed chicken and seasoning packet from the rice box. Stir to combine.
3. Add rice and chicken broth, lock the lid, and set the vent to sealing. Cook on high pressure for 5 minutes.
4. Once cooking finishes, let it stay on Keep Warm for 5 minutes, then quick-release the pressure.
5. Remove the lid and set the Instant Pot to Sauté again.
6. Stir in the skim milk, evaporated milk, and cream cheese until melted.
7. Mix the cornstarch with a little water to dissolve, then add to the soup to thicken. Stir well. Serve hot.

Classic French Onion Soup

Serves: 10 / Prep time: 10 minutes / Cook time: 20 minutes

Ingredients:
- ½ cup light margarine
- 8–10 large onions, sliced
- 3 (14-ounce) cans lower-sodium beef broth (98%

fat-free)
- 2½ cups water
- 3 teaspoons sodium-free chicken bouillon powder
- 1½ teaspoons Worcestershire sauce
- 3 bay leaves
- 10 (1-ounce) slices toasted French bread

Instructions:
1. Set the Instant Pot to Sauté mode, add margarine and onions, and cook for about 5 minutes until softened. Press Cancel to stop sautéing.
2. Add beef broth, water, bouillon powder, Worcestershire sauce, and bay leaves. Stir to combine.
3. Close the lid and set the vent to sealing. Cook on Manual for 20 minutes.
4. Allow the pressure to release naturally for 15 minutes, then quick-release any remaining steam. Remove bay leaves.
5. Ladle soup into bowls, topping each with a slice of toasted bread and cheese if desired.

Gigante Bean Soup with Celery and Kalamata Olives

Serves 6 to 8 / Prep time: 30 minutes / Cook time: 12 minutes

Ingredients:
- 1½ tablespoons table salt (for brining)
- 1 pound (454 g) dried gigante beans, rinsed and picked over
- 2 tablespoons extra-virgin olive oil (plus extra for drizzling)
- 5 celery ribs, cut into ½-inch pieces, plus ½ cup minced celery leaves
- 1 onion, chopped
- ½ teaspoon table salt
- 4 garlic cloves, minced
- 4 cups vegetable or chicken broth
- 4 cups water
- 2 bay leaves
- ½ cup pitted kalamata olives, chopped
- 2 tablespoons minced fresh marjoram or oregano
- Lemon wedges

Instructions:
1. In a large container, dissolve 1½ tablespoons salt in 2 quarts cold water. Add the beans and soak at room temperature for 8–24 hours. Drain and rinse.
2. Use the Sauté function on high in the Instant Pot. Heat olive oil and sauté the celery, onion, and ½ teaspoon salt for about 5 minutes until softened. Add garlic and cook until fragrant for 30 seconds. Stir in the broth, water, beans, and bay leaves.
3. Secure the lid, close the vent, and cook on high pressure for 6 minutes. Let the pressure release naturally for 15 minutes, then quick-release any remaining pressure. Carefully open the lid.

4. Mix the celery leaves, olives, and marjoram in a bowl. Discard bay leaves. Season with salt and pepper to taste. Serve soup topped with the celery-olive mixture, drizzled with extra olive oil, and a wedge of lemon.

Feta and Broccoli Soup

Serves: 4 / Prep time: 10 minutes / Cook time: 25 minutes

Ingredients:
- 1 cup chopped broccoli
- ½ cup coconut cream
- 1 teaspoon unsweetened tomato purée
- 4 cups beef broth
- 1 teaspoon chili flakes
- 6 ounces (170 g) crumbled feta

Instructions:
1. Place the chopped broccoli, coconut cream, tomato purée, and beef broth into the Instant Pot. Sprinkle chili flakes over the mixture and stir to combine.
2. Secure the lid and set the Instant Pot to Manual mode, adjusting to 8 minutes on High Pressure.
3. Once the timer goes off, perform a quick release of the pressure and open the lid.
4. Stir in the crumbled feta and switch the pot to Sauté mode, cooking for 5 minutes until the cheese fully melts.
5. Serve the soup while hot.

Chicken and Swiss Chard Soup

Serves: 4 / Prep time: 10 minutes / Cook time: 5 minutes

Ingredients:
- 1 chopped onion
- 6 garlic cloves
- 1 (2-inch) piece fresh ginger, chopped
- 1 (10-ounce / 283-g) can tomatoes with chiles
- 1½ cups full-fat coconut milk (divided)
- 1 tablespoon powdered chicken broth base
- 1 pound (454 g) boneless chicken thighs, cut into chunks
- 1½ cups chopped celery
- 2 cups chopped Swiss chard
- 1 teaspoon ground turmeric

Instructions:
1. In a blender, combine the onion, garlic, ginger, tomatoes, ½ cup coconut milk, and chicken broth base. Blend until smooth.
2. Transfer the purée into the Instant Pot, adding the chicken, celery, and Swiss chard.
3. Lock the lid and set to high pressure for 5 minutes. After cooking, let the pressure release naturally for 10 minutes before performing a quick release for any remaining pressure.
4. Open the lid, add the remaining coconut milk and turmeric, and stir to combine. Serve warm.

Italian Beef Meatball Soup

Serves: 6 / Prep time: 5 minutes / Cook time: 35 minutes

Ingredients:

- 1 pound (454 g) ground beef
- 1 large egg
- 1½ tablespoons flaxseed meal
- ⅓ cup shredded mozzarella cheese
- ¼ cup unsweetened tomato purée
- 1½ tablespoons Italian seasoning (divided)
- 1½ teaspoons garlic powder (divided)
- 1½ teaspoons salt (divided)
- 1 tablespoon olive oil
- 2 minced garlic cloves
- ½ medium yellow onion, minced
- ¼ cup pancetta, diced
- 1 cup sliced yellow squash
- 1 cup sliced zucchini
- ½ cup sliced turnips
- 4 cups beef broth
- 14 ounces (397 g) diced tomatoes
- ½ teaspoon ground black pepper
- 3 tablespoons grated Parmesan cheese

Instructions:

1. Preheat your oven to 400°F (205°C) and prepare a baking sheet with foil.
2. In a mixing bowl, combine the ground beef, egg, flaxseed meal, mozzarella, tomato purée, ½ tablespoon Italian seasoning, ½ teaspoon garlic powder, and ½ teaspoon salt. Mix thoroughly.
3. Shape the beef mixture into meatballs and place them on the baking sheet. Bake for 15 minutes, then set aside.
4. Set the Instant Pot to Sauté mode. Heat olive oil and sauté garlic, onion, and pancetta for 2 minutes until fragrant.
5. Add yellow squash, zucchini, and turnips to the pot and sauté for an additional 3 minutes.
6. Stir in beef broth, diced tomatoes, black pepper, and the remaining garlic powder, Italian seasoning, and salt. Add the baked meatballs to the mixture.
7. Lock the lid into place, set the Instant Pot to high pressure, and cook for 15 minutes.
8. Once cooking is complete, allow the pressure to release naturally for 10 minutes, then perform a quick release.
9. Gently stir the soup, then serve in bowls, topped with Parmesan cheese.

Chicken Enchilada Soup

Serves: 6 / Prep time: 10 minutes / Cook time: 40 minutes

Ingredients:

- 2 (6-ounce / 170-g) boneless, skinless chicken breasts
- ½ tablespoon chili powder
- ½ teaspoon salt
- ½ teaspoon garlic powder
- ¼ teaspoon pepper
- ½ cup red enchilada sauce
- ½ medium onion, diced
- 1 (4-ounce / 113-g) can green chilies
- 2 cups chicken broth
- ⅛ cup pickled jalapeños
- 4 ounces (113 g) cream cheese
- 1 cup uncooked cauliflower rice
- 1 avocado, diced
- 1 cup shredded mild Cheddar cheese
- ½ cup sour cream

Instructions:

1. Sprinkle seasoning over chicken breasts and set aside. Pour enchilada sauce into the Instant Pot and place chicken on top.
2. Add onion, chilies, broth, and jalapeños to the pot, then place cream cheese on top of the chicken. Close the lid and set the timer for 25 minutes.
3. Once the timer goes off, quick-release the pressure and shred the chicken with forks.
4. Mix the soup and add cauliflower rice, leaving the pot on Keep Warm mode. Replace the lid and let it sit for 15 minutes to cook the cauliflower rice.
5. Serve with avocado, Cheddar cheese, and sour cream.

Beef Oxtail Soup with White Beans, Tomatoes, and Aleppo Pepper

Serves: 6 to 8 / Prep time: 20 minutes / Cook time: 1 hour 10 minutes

Ingredients:

- 4 pounds (1.8 kg) oxtails, trimmed
- 1 teaspoon table salt
- 1 tablespoon extra-virgin olive oil
- 1 onion, chopped fine
- 2 carrots, peeled and chopped fine
- ¼ cup ground dried Aleppo pepper
- 6 garlic cloves, minced
- 2 tablespoons tomato paste
- ¾ teaspoon dried oregano
- ½ teaspoon ground cinnamon
- ½ teaspoon ground cumin
- 6 cups water
- 1 (28-ounce / 794-g) can diced tomatoes, drained
- 1 (15-ounce / 425-g) can navy beans, rinsed
- 1 tablespoon sherry vinegar
- ¼ cup chopped fresh parsley
- ½ preserved lemon, pulp and white pith removed, rind rinsed and minced (2 tablespoons)

Instructions:

1. Pat oxtails dry with paper towels and sprinkle with salt. Heat oil on the highest sauté setting for 5 minutes (until

just smoking). Brown half of the oxtails, 4 to 6 minutes per side, then set aside.

2. Add onion and carrots to the pot and cook until softened, about 5 minutes. Stir in Aleppo pepper, garlic, tomato paste, oregano, cinnamon, and cumin, cooking for 30 seconds.
3. Stir in water, scraping up any browned bits, and add tomatoes. Add the remaining uncooked oxtails with any accumulated juices.
4. Lock the lid in place, close the pressure release valve, and set to high pressure for 45 minutes. After cooking, quick-release the pressure.
5. Carefully remove the oxtails and shred the meat with forks, discarding the bones and fat. Strain the broth and return it to the pot.
6. Stir in the shredded oxtails and beans. Cook on the highest sauté function for 5 minutes, stirring in vinegar and parsley.
7. Serve, passing preserved lemon separately.

Salmon and Tomatillos Stew

Serves: 2 / Prep time: 15 minutes / Cook time: 12 minutes

Ingredients:
- 10 ounces (283 g) salmon fillet, chopped
- 2 tomatillos, chopped
- ½ teaspoon ground turmeric
- 1 cup coconut cream
- 1 teaspoon ground paprika
- ½ teaspoon salt

Instructions:
1. Place all Ingredients in the Instant Pot and stir to combine.
2. Close the lid and set to Manual mode, cooking for 12 minutes on Low Pressure.
3. Once the timer beeps, quick-release the pressure and open the lid.
4. Serve warm.

Pasta e Fagioli with Ground Beef

Serves: 8 / Prep time: 0 minutes / Cook time: 30 minutes

Ingredients:
- 2 tablespoons extra-virgin olive oil
- 4 garlic cloves, minced
- 1 yellow onion, diced
- 2 large carrots, diced
- 4 celery stalks, diced
- 1½ pounds 95 percent extra-lean ground beef
- 4 cups low-sodium vegetable broth
- 2 teaspoons Italian seasoning
- ½ teaspoon freshly ground black pepper
- 1¼ cups chickpea-based elbow pasta or whole-wheat elbow pasta
- 1½ cups drained cooked kidney beans, or one

- 15-ounce can kidney beans, rinsed and drained
- One 28-ounce can whole San Marzano tomatoes and their liquid
- 2 tablespoons chopped fresh flat-leaf parsley

Instructions:
1. Select the Sauté setting and heat the oil and garlic for 2 minutes, until the garlic is bubbling but not browned. Add the onion, carrots, and celery and sauté for 5 minutes until softened.
2. Add the ground beef and sauté for 5 minutes, breaking it up as it cooks, until it is no longer pink.
3. Stir in the broth, Italian seasoning, black pepper, and pasta, making sure the pasta is submerged. Add the beans and tomatoes, crushing the tomatoes with your hands as you add them.
4. Secure the lid and set the Pressure Release to Sealing. Set the Instant Pot to Pressure Cook on low for 2 minutes.
5. Once the cooking time ends, let the pressure release naturally for 10 minutes, then quick-release any remaining steam.
6. Stir the soup to combine, and serve with a sprinkle of parsley.

Asparagus and Chicken Coconut Soup

Serves: 8 / Prep time: 7 minutes / Cook time: 11 minutes

Ingredients:
- 1 tablespoon unsalted butter (or coconut oil for dairy-free)
- ¼ cup finely chopped onions
- 2 cloves garlic, minced
- 1 (14-ounce / 397-g) can full-fat coconut milk
- 1 (14-ounce / 397-g) can sugar-free tomato sauce
- 1 cup chicken broth
- 1 tablespoon red curry paste
- 1 teaspoon fine sea salt
- ½ teaspoon ground black pepper
- 2 pounds (907 g) boneless, skinless chicken breasts, cut into ½-inch chunks
- 2 cups asparagus, trimmed and cut into 2-inch pieces
- Fresh cilantro leaves, for garnish
- Lime wedges, for garnish

Instructions:
1. Place the butter in the Instant Pot and press Sauté. Once melted, add onions and garlic and sauté for 4 minutes, or until the onions soften. Press Cancel to stop Sauté.
2. Add coconut milk, tomato sauce, broth, curry paste, salt, and pepper. Whisk well to combine. Stir in chicken and asparagus.
3. Seal the lid, press Manual, and set the timer for 7 minutes. Once finished, turn the valve to venting for a quick release.
4. Remove the lid and stir well. Taste and adjust

seasoning. Ladle the soup into bowls and garnish with cilantro. Serve with lime wedges or a squirt of lime juice.

Turkey and Barley Vegetable Soup

Serves: 8 / Prep time: 5 minutes / Cook time: 20 minutes

Ingredients:
- 2 tablespoons avocado oil
- 1 pound ground turkey
- 4 cups Chicken Bone Broth, low-sodium store-bought chicken broth, or water
- 1 (28-ounce) carton or can diced tomatoes
- 2 tablespoons tomato paste
- 1 (15-ounce) package frozen chopped carrots (about 2½ cups)
- 1 (15-ounce) package frozen peppers and onions (about 2½ cups)
- ⅓ cup dry barley
- 1 teaspoon kosher salt
- ¼ teaspoon freshly ground black pepper
- 2 bay leaves

Instructions:
1. Set the electric pressure cooker to Sauté/More. When hot, pour in the avocado oil.
2. Add turkey and sauté, breaking it up frequently, for about 7 minutes until no longer pink. Press Cancel.
3. Add broth, tomatoes, tomato paste, carrots, peppers, onions, barley, salt, pepper, and bay leaves.
4. Close and lock the lid, setting the valve to sealing.
5. Cook on high pressure for 20 minutes.
6. When the timer goes off, press Cancel and allow the pressure to release naturally for 10 minutes. Then, quick-release any remaining pressure.
7. Once the pin drops, unlock and remove the lid. Discard the bay leaves.
8. Spoon into bowls and serve.

Spanish-Style Turkey Meatball Soup

Serves: 6-8 / Prep time: 10 minutes / Cook time: 15 minutes

Ingredients:
- 1 slice hearty white sandwich bread, torn into quarters
- ¼ cup whole milk
- 1 ounce (28 g) Manchego cheese, grated (½ cup), plus extra for serving
- 5 tablespoons minced fresh parsley, divided
- ½ teaspoon table salt
- 1 pound (454 g) ground turkey
- 1 tablespoon extra-virgin olive oil
- 1 onion, chopped
- 1 red bell pepper, stemmed, seeded, and cut into ¾-inch pieces
- 4 garlic cloves, minced

- 2 teaspoons smoked paprika
- ½ cup dry white wine
- 8 cups chicken broth
- 8 ounces (227 g) kale, stemmed and chopped

Instructions:
1. Mash bread and milk into a paste in a large bowl using a fork. Stir in Manchego, 3 tablespoons parsley, and salt. Add turkey and knead the mixture with your hands until well combined. Roll the mixture into 2-teaspoon-sized meatballs (about 35 meatballs) and set aside.
2. Heat oil in the Instant Pot on the highest sauté setting until shimmering. Add onion and bell pepper and cook until softened and lightly browned, about 5-7 minutes. Stir in garlic and paprika and cook until fragrant, about 30 seconds. Stir in wine, scraping up any browned bits, and cook until almost evaporated, about 5 minutes. Stir in broth and kale, then gently submerge meatballs.
3. Lock the lid in place and close the pressure release valve. Select high pressure and cook for 3 minutes.
4. Turn off the Instant Pot and quick-release pressure. Carefully remove the lid, allowing steam to escape away from you.
5. Stir in remaining parsley and season with salt and pepper to taste. Serve with extra Manchego on the side.

Rich and Creamy Mushroom Soup

Serves: 4 / Prep time: 10 minutes / Cook time: 10 minutes

Ingredients:
- 1 pound (454 g) sliced button mushrooms
- 3 tablespoons butter
- 2 tablespoons diced onion
- 2 cloves garlic, minced
- 2 cups chicken broth
- ½ teaspoon salt
- ¼ teaspoon pepper
- ½ cup heavy cream
- ¼ teaspoon xanthan gum

Instructions:
1. Press the Sauté button, then press Adjust to set heat to Less. Add mushrooms, butter, and onion to the pot. Sauté for 5-8 minutes until onions and mushrooms begin to brown. Add garlic and sauté until fragrant. Press Cancel.
2. Add broth, salt, and pepper. Close the lid, press Manual, and set the timer for 3 minutes. When the timer beeps, quick-release the pressure.
3. Stir in the heavy cream and xanthan gum. Let it thicken for a few minutes and serve warm.

Avocado and Serrano Chile Delight Soup

Serves: 4 / Prep time: 10 minutes / Cook time: 7 minutes

Ingredients:
- 2 avocados

- 1 small fresh tomatillo, quartered
- 2 cups chicken broth
- 2 tablespoons avocado oil
- 1 tablespoon butter
- 2 tablespoons finely minced onion
- 1 clove garlic, minced
- ½ Serrano chile, deseeded and ribs removed, minced, plus thin slices for garnish
- ¼ teaspoon sea salt
- Pinch of ground white pepper
- ½ cup full-fat coconut milk
- Fresh cilantro sprigs, for garnish

Instructions:

1. Scoop the avocado flesh into a food processor. Add tomatillo and chicken broth. Purée until smooth, then set aside.
2. Set the Instant Pot to Sauté mode and add avocado oil and butter. When the butter melts, add onion and garlic and sauté for 1 minute until softened. Add Serrano chile and sauté for 1 more minute.
3. Pour in the avocado mixture, add salt and pepper, and stir to combine.
4. Secure the lid and press Manual. Set the cooking time for 5 minutes on High Pressure.
5. When the timer beeps, use a quick pressure release. Open the lid and stir in coconut milk.
6. Serve hot, garnished with thin slices of Serrano chile and cilantro sprigs.

Creamy Blue Cheese Mushroom Soup

Serves: 4 / Prep time: 15 minutes / Cook time: 20 minutes

Ingredients:

- 2 cups chopped white mushrooms
- 3 tablespoons cream cheese
- 4 ounces (113 g) scallions, diced
- 4 cups chicken broth
- 1 teaspoon olive oil
- ½ teaspoon ground cumin
- 1 teaspoon salt
- 2 ounces (57 g) blue cheese, crumbled

Instructions:

1. Combine mushrooms, cream cheese, scallions, chicken broth, olive oil, and ground cumin in the Instant Pot.
2. Seal the lid and select Manual mode, setting the cooking time for 20 minutes on High Pressure.
3. When the timer beeps, use a quick pressure release and open the lid.
4. Add salt and blend the soup with an immersion blender.
5. Ladle the soup into bowls and top with crumbled blue cheese. Serve warm.

Cabbage Roll Soup with Pork and Beef

Serves: 4 / Prep time: 10 minutes / Cook time: 8 minutes

Ingredients:

- ½ pound (227 g) 84% lean ground pork
- ½ pound (227 g) 85% lean ground beef
- ½ medium onion, diced
- ½ medium head cabbage, thinly sliced
- 2 tablespoons sugar-free tomato paste
- ½ cup diced tomatoes
- 2 cups chicken broth
- 1 teaspoon salt
- ½ teaspoon thyme
- ½ teaspoon garlic powder
- ¼ teaspoon pepper

Instructions:

1. Press the Sauté button and add beef and pork to the Instant Pot. Brown the meat until no pink remains. Add the onion and cook until fragrant and soft. Press Cancel.
2. Add the remaining Ingredients to the Instant Pot. Press the Manual button and set the time for 8 minutes.
3. When the timer beeps, allow a 15-minute natural release, then quick-release the remaining pressure. Serve warm.

Mushroom and Root Vegetable Beef Stew

Serves: 6 / Prep time: 0 minutes / Cook time: 55 minutes

Ingredients:

- 1½ pounds beef stew meat
- ¾ teaspoon fine sea salt
- ¾ teaspoon freshly ground black pepper
- 1 tablespoon cold-pressed avocado oil
- 3 garlic cloves, minced
- 1 yellow onion, diced
- 2 celery stalks, diced
- 8 ounces cremini mushrooms, quartered
- 1 cup low-sodium roasted beef bone broth
- 2 tablespoons Worcestershire sauce
- 1 tablespoon Dijon mustard
- 1 teaspoon dried rosemary, crumbled
- 1 bay leaf
- 3 tablespoons tomato paste
- 8 ounces carrots, cut into 1-inch-thick rounds
- 1 pound turnips, cut into 1-inch pieces
- 1 pound parsnips, halved lengthwise, then cut crosswise into 1-inch pieces

Instructions:

1. Sprinkle the beef with salt and pepper.
2. Select the Sauté setting on the Instant Pot. Heat oil and garlic for 2 minutes, until the garlic is bubbling but not browned. Add the onion, celery, and mushrooms and sauté for 5 minutes, until softened. Stir in the broth, Worcestershire sauce, mustard, rosemary, and bay leaf. Add the beef and top with tomato paste. Do not stir.

3. Secure the lid, set the Pressure Release to Sealing, and press Cancel. Select Meat/Stew or Pressure Cook and set the time for 20 minutes on high pressure.
4. When the cooking program ends, perform a quick pressure release or let the pressure release naturally. Discard the bay leaf and stir in the tomato paste.
5. Add carrots, turnips, and parsnips on top of the meat. Secure the lid, set the Pressure Release to Sealing, and press Cancel. Select Pressure Cook and set the time for 3 minutes on low pressure.
6. When the cooking program ends, perform a quick pressure release. Stir to combine.
7. Ladle the stew into bowls and serve hot.

Jalapeño Pancetta Soup

Serves: 4 / Prep time: 10 minutes / Cook time: 10 minutes

Ingredients:
- 3 ounces (85 g) pancetta, chopped
- 1 teaspoon coconut oil
- 2 jalapeño peppers, sliced
- ½ teaspoon garlic powder
- ½ teaspoon smoked paprika
- ½ cup heavy cream
- 2 cups water
- ½ cup Monterey Jack cheese, shredded

Instructions:
1. Add pancetta to the Instant Pot, then add coconut oil and cook on Sauté mode for 4 minutes, stirring constantly.
2. Add sliced jalapeños, garlic powder, and smoked paprika. Sauté for 1 more minute.
3. Pour in heavy cream and water. Add Monterey Jack cheese and stir to mix well.
4. Close the lid, select Manual mode, and set the cooking time on High Pressure.
5. When the timer beeps, use a quick pressure release and open the lid.
6. Serve warm.

Mushroom and Sausage Pizza Soup

Serves: 3 / Prep time: 10 minutes / Cook time: 22 minutes

Ingredients:
- 1 teaspoon coconut oil
- ¼ cup cremini mushrooms, sliced
- 5 ounces (142 g) Italian sausages, chopped
- ½ jalapeño pepper, sliced
- ½ teaspoon Italian seasoning
- 1 teaspoon unsweetened tomato purée
- 1 cup water
- 4 ounces (113 g) Mozzarella, shredded

Instructions:
1. Melt coconut oil in the Instant Pot on Sauté mode.
2. Add mushrooms and cook for 10 minutes.

3. Add chopped sausages, jalapeño, Italian seasoning, and tomato purée. Pour in the water and mix well.
4. Close the lid, select Manual mode, and set the cooking time for 12 minutes on High Pressure.
5. After the timer beeps, quick-release the pressure and open the lid.
6. Ladle the soup into bowls and top with Mozzarella. Serve warm.

Spiced Carrot Soup with Greek Yogurt

Serves: 6 to 8 / Prep time: 15 minutes / Cook time: 10 minutes

Ingredients:
- 2 tablespoons extra-virgin olive oil
- 2 onions, chopped
- 1 teaspoon table salt
- 1 tablespoon grated fresh ginger
- 1 tablespoon ground coriander
- 1 tablespoon ground fennel
- 1 teaspoon ground cinnamon
- 4 cups vegetable or chicken broth
- 2 cups water
- 2 pounds (907 g) carrots, peeled and cut into 2-inch pieces
- ½ teaspoon baking soda
- 2 tablespoons pomegranate molasses
- ½ cup plain Greek yogurt
- ½ cup hazelnuts, toasted, skinned, and chopped
- ½ cup chopped fresh cilantro or mint

Instructions:
1. Heat oil in the Instant Pot on the highest sauté setting until shimmering. Add onions and salt and cook for about 5 minutes, until softened. Stir in ginger, coriander, fennel, and cinnamon, cooking for 30 seconds.
2. Add broth, water, carrots, and baking soda. Lock the lid in place, close the pressure release valve, and select high pressure cook for 3 minutes. Quick-release the pressure once done.
3. Carefully remove the lid and process the soup in batches in a blender until smooth. Return the soup to the Instant Pot and simmer on high sauté.
4. Season with salt and pepper to taste. Drizzle with pomegranate molasses and top with yogurt, hazelnuts, and cilantro or mint before serving.

Eggplant and Potato Beef Stew

Serves: 6-8 / Prep time: 15 minutes / Cook time: 50 minutes

Ingredients:
- 2 pounds (907 g) boneless short ribs, trimmed and cut into 1-inch pieces
- 1½ teaspoons table salt, divided

- 2 tablespoons extra-virgin olive oil
- 1 onion, chopped
- 3 tablespoons tomato paste
- ¼ cup all-purpose flour
- 3 garlic cloves, minced
- 1 tablespoon ground cumin
- 1 teaspoon ground turmeric
- 1 teaspoon ground cardamom
- ¾ teaspoon ground cinnamon
- 4 cups chicken broth
- 1 cup water
- 1 pound (454 g) eggplant, cut into 1-inch pieces
- 1 pound (454 g) Yukon Gold potatoes, unpeeled, cut into 1-inch pieces
- ½ cup chopped fresh mint or parsley

Instructions:

1. Pat the beef dry with paper towels and sprinkle with 1 teaspoon salt. Heat oil in the Instant Pot on the highest sauté setting for 5 minutes or until smoking. Brown half of the beef for 7-9 minutes on all sides, then transfer to a bowl. Set aside the remaining uncooked beef.
2. Add onion to the pot and cook for 5 minutes until softened. Stir in tomato paste, flour, garlic, cumin, turmeric, cardamom, cinnamon, and the remaining ½ teaspoon salt. Cook until fragrant, about 1 minute. Gradually whisk in broth and water, scraping up any browned bits. Stir in eggplant and potatoes, then nestle the remaining uncooked beef into the pot along with the browned beef and its juices.
3. Lock the lid in place and set the pressure release valve to sealing. Cook on high pressure for 30 minutes.
4. After cooking, quick-release the pressure carefully.
5. Skim excess fat from the surface using a spoon. Stir in mint and season with salt and pepper to taste.
6. Serve warm.

Hearty Vegetarian Chili

Serves: 6 / Prep time: 25 minutes / Cook time: 10 minutes

Ingredients:

- 2 teaspoons olive oil
- 3 garlic cloves, minced
- 2 onions, chopped
- 1 green bell pepper, chopped
- 1 cup textured vegetable protein (T.V.P.)
- 1-pound can beans of your choice, drained
- 1 jalapeño pepper, seeds removed, chopped
- 28-ounce can diced Italian tomatoes
- 1 bay leaf
- 1 tablespoon dried oregano
- ½ teaspoon salt
- ¼ teaspoon pepper

Instructions:

1. Set the Instant Pot to the Sauté function. Add olive oil, garlic, onions, and bell pepper. Stir for about 5 minutes as the mixture cooks. Press Cancel.
2. Add the remaining Ingredients to the inner pot and stir.
3. Secure the lid, set the vent to sealing, and cook on Manual mode for 10 minutes.
4. Once the cooking time is done, let the steam release naturally for 5 minutes, then manually release the rest.

Creamy Jalapeño Popper Chicken Soup

Serves: 4 / Prep time: 5 minutes / Cook time: 25 minutes

Ingredients:

- 2 tablespoons butter
- ½ medium diced onion
- ¼ cup sliced pickled jalapeños
- ¼ cup cooked crumbled bacon
- 2 cups chicken broth
- 2 cups cooked diced chicken
- 4 ounces (113 g) cream cheese
- 1 teaspoon salt
- ½ teaspoon pepper
- ¼ teaspoon garlic powder
- ⅓ cup heavy cream
- 1 cup shredded sharp Cheddar cheese

Instructions:

1. Press the Sauté button. Add butter, onion, and sliced jalapeños to the Instant Pot. Sauté for 5 minutes, until onions are translucent. Add bacon and press Cancel.
2. Add broth, chicken, cream cheese, salt, pepper, and garlic powder. Close the lid. Press the Soup button and adjust the time to 20 minutes.
3. When the timer goes off, quick-release the steam. Stir in the heavy cream and Cheddar cheese. Continue stirring until the cheese is fully melted. Serve warm.

Unstuffed Cabbage and Rice Soup

Serves: 5 / Prep time: 15 minutes / Cook time: 20 minutes

Ingredients:

- 2 tablespoons coconut oil
- 1 pound ground sirloin or turkey
- 1 medium onion, diced
- 2 cloves garlic, minced
- 1 small head cabbage, chopped, cored, and cut into roughly 2-inch pieces
- 6-ounce can low-sodium tomato paste
- 32-ounce can low-sodium diced tomatoes, with liquid
- 2 cups low-sodium beef broth
- 1½ cups water
- ¾ cup brown rice
- 1–2 teaspoons salt
- ½ teaspoon black pepper
- 1 teaspoon oregano
- 1 teaspoon parsley

Instructions:

1. Melt coconut oil in the Instant Pot using the Sauté function. Add the ground meat and cook until it loses color, about 2 minutes.
2. Add onions and garlic and sauté for 2 more minutes, stirring frequently.
3. Add the chopped cabbage to the pot.
4. Top with tomato paste, tomatoes with liquid, beef broth, water, rice, and spices.
5. Secure the lid, set the vent to sealing, and cook on Manual mode for 20 minutes.
6. Once the time is up, allow the pressure to release naturally for 10 minutes, then quick-release any remaining pressure.

Poblano Chicken Soup

Serves: 8 / Prep time: 10 minutes / Cook time: 20 minutes

Ingredients:

- 1 cup diced onion
- 3 poblano peppers, chopped
- 5 garlic cloves
- 2 cups diced cauliflower
- 1½ pounds (680 g) chicken breast, cut into large chunks
- ¼ cup chopped fresh cilantro
- 1 teaspoon ground coriander
- 1 teaspoon ground cumin
- 1 to 2 teaspoons salt
- 2 cups water
- 2 ounces (57 g) cream cheese, cut into small chunks
- 1 cup sour cream

Instructions:

1. In the Instant Pot, add the onion, poblanos, garlic, cauliflower, chicken, cilantro, coriander, cumin, salt, and water.
2. Secure the lid and set to Manual mode on High. Cook for 15 minutes. Let the pressure release naturally for 10 minutes, then quick-release any remaining pressure. Open the lid.
3. Use tongs to remove the chicken and place it in a bowl.
4. Tilt the pot and use an immersion blender to roughly purée the vegetable mixture, leaving it slightly chunky.
5. Set the Instant Pot to Sauté mode on high. Once the broth is bubbling, add the cream cheese and stir until melted. If needed, whisk to fully incorporate the cream cheese.
6. Shred the chicken and return it to the pot. Stir until heated through, then serve topped with sour cream.

Mushroom and Beef Wild Rice Soup

Serves: 6 / Prep time: 0 minutes / Cook time: 55 minutes

Ingredients:

- 2 tablespoons extra-virgin olive oil or unsalted butter
- 2 garlic cloves, minced
- 8 ounces shiitake mushrooms, stems removed and sliced
- 1 teaspoon fine sea salt
- 2 carrots, diced
- 2 celery stalks, diced
- 1 yellow onion, diced
- 1 teaspoon dried thyme
- 1½ pounds beef stew meat, cut into ¾-inch pieces
- 4 cups low-sodium roasted beef bone broth
- 1 cup wild rice, rinsed
- 1 tablespoon Worcestershire sauce
- 2 tablespoons tomato paste

Instructions:

1. Set the Instant Pot to Sauté mode. Heat the oil and garlic for 1 minute, until the garlic is bubbling but not browned. Add the mushrooms and salt and sauté for 5 minutes until the mushrooms release their liquid.
2. Add the carrots, celery, and onion, then sauté for 4 minutes until the onion softens. Add the thyme and beef, and sauté for an additional 3 minutes until the beef is mostly opaque.
3. Stir in the broth, rice, Worcestershire sauce, and tomato paste, scraping up any browned bits from the bottom.
4. Secure the lid and set to Pressure Cook on High for 25 minutes. After the cook time ends, let the pressure release naturally for 15 minutes, then move the pressure release valve to Venting.
5. Open the lid and ladle the soup into bowls. Serve hot.

Green Chile Corn Chowder

Serves: 8 / Prep time: 20 minutes / Cook time: 7 to 8 hours

Ingredients:

- 16-ounce can cream-style corn
- 3 potatoes, peeled and diced
- 2 tablespoons chopped fresh chives
- 4-ounce can diced green chilies, drained
- 2-ounce jar chopped pimentos, drained
- ½ cup chopped cooked ham
- 2 10½-ounce cans 100% fat-free lower-sodium chicken broth
- Pepper to taste
- Tabasco sauce, to taste
- 1 cup fat-free milk

Instructions:

1. In the Instant Pot, combine all Ingredients except for the milk.
2. Secure the lid and set to Slow Cook on low for 7-8 hours, or until the potatoes are tender.
3. Once the cooking time is complete, stir in the milk. Cover and let simmer for another 20 minutes.

MEASUREMENT CONVERSION CHART

VOLUME EQUIVALENTS(DRY)

US STANDARD	METRIC (APPROXIMATE)
1/8 teaspoon	0.5 mL
1/4 teaspoon	1 mL
1/2 teaspoon	2 mL
3/4 teaspoon	4 mL
1 teaspoon	5 mL
1 tablespoon	15 mL
1/4 cup	59 mL
1/2 cup	118 mL
3/4 cup	177 mL
1 cup	235 mL
2 cups	475 mL
3 cups	700 mL
4 cups	1 L

VOLUME EQUIVALENTS(LIQUID)

US STANDARD	US STANDARD (OUNCES)	METRIC (APPROXIMATE)
2 tablespoons	1 fl.oz.	30 mL
1/4 cup	2 fl.oz.	60 mL
1/2 cup	4 fl.oz.	120 mL
1 cup	8 fl.oz.	240 mL
1 1/2 cup	12 fl.oz.	355 mL
2 cups or 1 pint	16 fl.oz.	475 mL
4 cups or 1 quart	32 fl.oz.	1 L
1 gallon	128 fl.oz.	4 L

TEMPERATURES EQUIVALENTS

FAHRENHEIT(F)	CELSIUS(C) (APPROXIMATE)
225 °F	107 °C
250 °F	120 °C
275 °F	135 °C
300 °F	150 °C
325 °F	160 °C
350 °F	180 °C
375 °F	190 °C
400 °F	205 °C
425 °F	220 °C
450 °F	235 °C
475 °F	245 °C
500 °F	260 °C

WEIGHT EQUIVALENTS

US STANDARD	METRIC (APPROXIMATE)
1 ounce	28 g
2 ounces	57 g
5 ounces	142 g
10 ounces	284 g
15 ounces	425 g
16 ounces (1 pound)	455 g
1.5 pounds	680 g
2 pounds	907 g

The Dirty Dozen and Clean Fifteen

The Environmental Working Group (EWG) is a nonprofit, nonpartisan organization dedicated to protecting human health and the environment Its mission is to empower people to live healthier lives in a healthier environment. This organization publishes an annual list of the twelve kinds of produce, in sequence, that have the highest amount of pesticide residue-the Dirty Dozen-as well as a list of the fifteen kinds ofproduce that have the least amount of pesticide residue-the Clean Fifteen.

THE DIRTY DOZEN

- The 2016 Dirty Dozen includes the following produce. These are considered among the year's most important produce to buy organic:

Strawberries	Spinach
Apples	Tomatoes
Nectarines	Bell peppers
Peaches	Cherry tomatoes
Celery	Cucumbers
Grapes	Kale/collard greens
Cherries	Hot peppers

- *The Dirty Dozen list contains two additional itemskale/collard greens and hot peppers-because they tend to contain trace levels of highly hazardous pesticides.*

THE CLEAN FIFTEEN

- The least critical to buy organically are the Clean Fifteen list. The following are on the 2016 list:

Avocados	Papayas
Corn	Kiw
Pineapples	Eggplant
Cabbage	Honeydew
Sweet peas	Grapefruit
Onions	Cantaloupe
Asparagus	Cauliflower
Mangos	

- *Some of the sweet corn sold in the United States are made from genetically engineered (GE) seedstock. Buy organic varieties of these crops to avoid GE produce.*

INDEX

Made in United States
Troutdale, OR
12/17/2024